THE KEEPER

W9-CNH-056

"*The Keeper* is a triumph! Kelcey Ervick's rollicking visual storytelling makes this information-packed lesson in women's sports history both hilarious and surprisingly moving. Do not be deceived by her loose, exuberant drawings—the level of writerly control at play in this beautiful book is prodigious."

—Alison Bechdel, author of the *New York Times* bestselling
Fun Home and *The Secret to Superhuman Strength*

"I didn't know I'd be embarking on an adventure into history, pop culture, tender storytelling, and sharp wit when I started *The Keeper*. I know nothing about sports, but I was hanging on every word (and gorgeous drawing). Kelcey Ervick's story is fascinating and relatable for any of us who have ever journeyed into identity within the limiting structures of society, and she gives us a delightful road map for finding our own way. *The Keeper* is so entertaining and so moving that I wasn't sure if I should tear up or giggle on any given page, and so informative that I was left in total awe by the end."

—Mari Andrew, *New York Times* bestselling author of *Am I There Yet?*

"If Alison Bechdel were a goalkeeper, this is the memoir she would have written—dueling bitter and sweet, *The Keeper* is a feminist anthem and a writer's coming-of-age in a graphic disguise. It's a book for the athlete in your house—and maybe for the athlete you were told you couldn't really be."

—KJ Dell'Antonia, *New York Times* bestselling author of *The Chicken Sisters*

"I am so glad to have read this marvelous book. I loved drinking in the paintings and am so in awe of Ervick's artistry, and her amazing story as an athlete and writer, but also *The Keeper* helped me comprehend more deeply the women who organized and fought (and played soccer and took a knee) for rights and justice in our time. This book is profoundly great and necessary right now."

—Tom Hart, #1 *New York Times* bestselling author and illustrator
of *Rosalie Lightning: A Graphic Memoir*

"Kelcey Ervick's *The Keeper* offers a fascinating look at important figures through history who have pushed for equal standing for women in sports—a fight that continues today. But this book is also about sisterhood and the sacred bonds between teammates. It's about the love of the game and the deep sense of joy and power it provides. It's about the collective strength of women and how we have built on one another's achievements, one generation passing the baton to the next, to ensure a future without limits for the girls who will follow. *The Keeper* is equal parts inspiration and motivation."

—Briana Scurry, World Cup champion U.S. goalkeeper, two-time Olympic gold medalist, and author of *My Greatest Save*

"*The Keeper* is a winner. You don't have to be an athlete to appreciate this inspiring graphic memoir. Not only does it offer page after page of beautiful artwork, but *The Keeper* is a young woman's coming-of-age story, a history lesson, and a call to action. Kelcey Ervick accomplishes a magical feat found in the best of memoirs—she's depicted a life's journey that's completely original, while also making it feel universal. To say I loved this book is an understatement."

—Elise Hooper, author of *Fast Girls*

"*The Keeper* is a beautifully illustrated story about growing up in America. Part memoir, part essay, part archive, and part documentary, Ervick masterfully blends a moving coming-of-age story with an illuminating history of Title IX and women's access to sports. By examining old diaries, photographs, videos, and other ephemera, she generously shares her process of realizing the many aspects of her identity: athlete and artist, mother and writer, wife and individual. *The Keeper* is a timely work, full of heart."

—Margaret Kimball, author of *And Now I Spill the Family Secrets*

"Title IX changed everything, my mother says. She grew up in the fifties and resented that her two strongest points, academics and athletics, were pluses for boys and minuses for girls. Thankfully, things were different for author Kelcey Ervick, who shows us, in this beautifully written and drawn memoir, the huge leaps gained since then and how far we have to go, weaving together her personal history as a girls' soccer champion and the important, intertwined histories of women's athletics and women's civil rights."

—Ellen Forney, author of the *New York Times* bestselling *Marbles*

THE KEEPER

Soccer, Me, and the Law That Changed Women's Lives

Kelcey Ervick

AVERY
an imprint of Penguin Random House
New York

AVERY

an imprint of Penguin Random House LLC
penguinrandomhouse.com

Most Avery books are available at special quantity discounts for bulk purchase for sales promotions, premiums, fund-raising, and educational needs. Special books or book excerpts also can be created to fit specific needs. For details, write SpecialMarkets@penguinrandomhouse.com.

Library of Congress Cataloging-in-Publication Data
Names: Ervick, Kelcey, author, artist.
Title: The keeper: soccer, me, and the law that changed women's lives / Kelcey Ervick.
Description: New York: Avery, Penguin Random House, 2022.
Identifiers: LCCN 2022008272 (print) | LCCN 2022008273 (ebook) |
ISBN 9780593539187 (trade paperback) | ISBN 9780593539194 (epub)
Subjects: LCSH: Ervick, Kelcey—Comic books, strips, etc. | Women soccer players—United States—Biography—Comic books, strips, etc. | Soccer goalkeepers—United States—Biography—Comic books, strips, etc. | United States. Education Amendments of 1972. Title IX—Comic books, strips, etc. | Sex discrimination in sports—Law and legislation—United States—Comic books, strips, etc. | LCGFT: Sports comics. | Autobiographical comics. | Coming-of-age comics. | Graphic novels.
Classification: LCC GV942.7.E79 A3 2022 (print) | LCC GV942.7.E79 (ebook) |
DDC 796.334092 [B]—dc23/eng/20220608
LC record available at https://lccn.loc.gov/2022008272
LC ebook record available at https://lccn.loc.gov/2022008273

Printed in the United States of America
1st Printing

Book composition by Lorie Pagnozzi

For Jake
(for keeps)

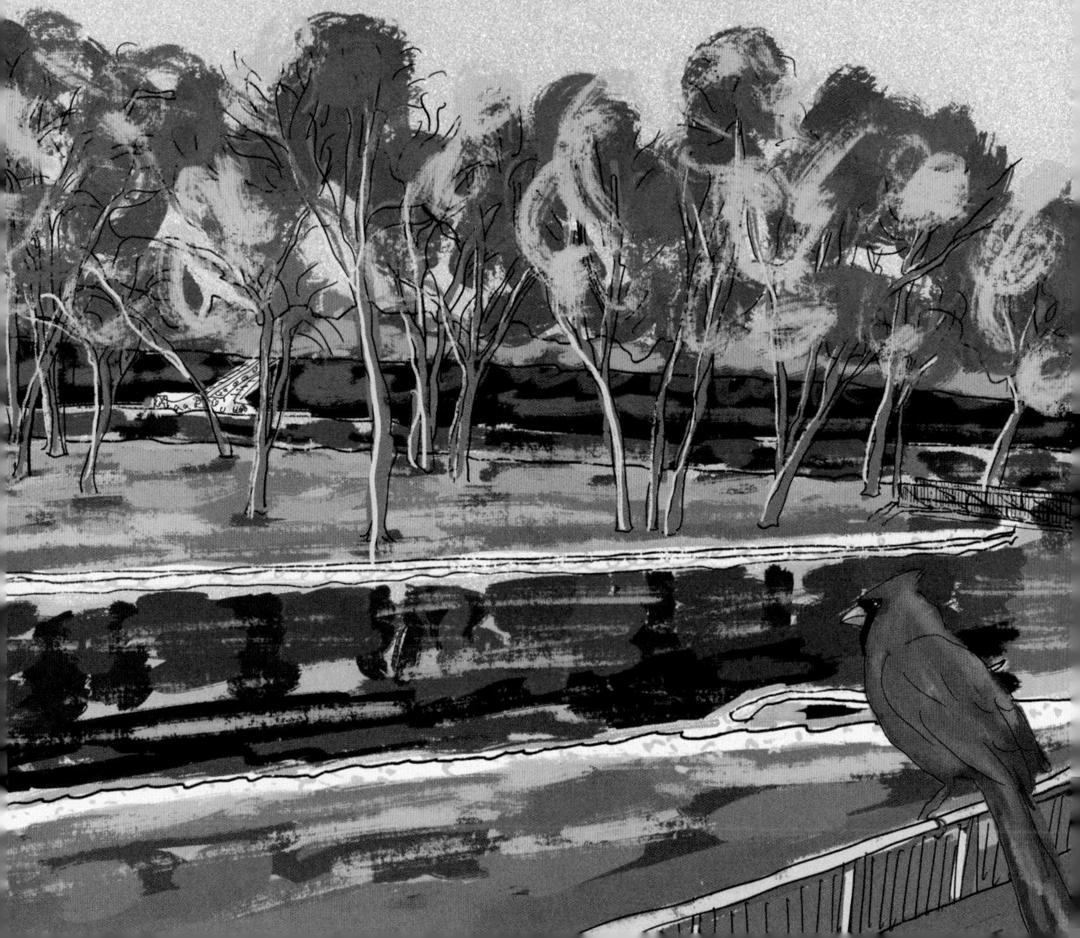

TABLE OF

KEE

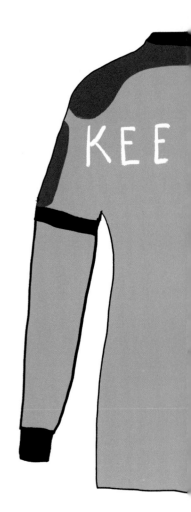

CONTENTS

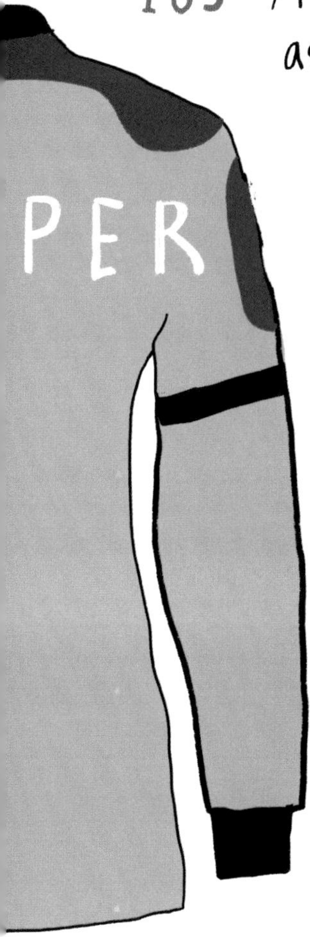
PER

"I was less the KEEPER of a SOCCER GOAL than the KEEPER of a SECRET."

— Vladimir Nabokov, SPEAK, MEMORY

"It wasn't just SOCCER that exploded...it was POWERFUL WOMEN."

—Briana Scurry,
USWNT GOALKEEPER, 1994–2008

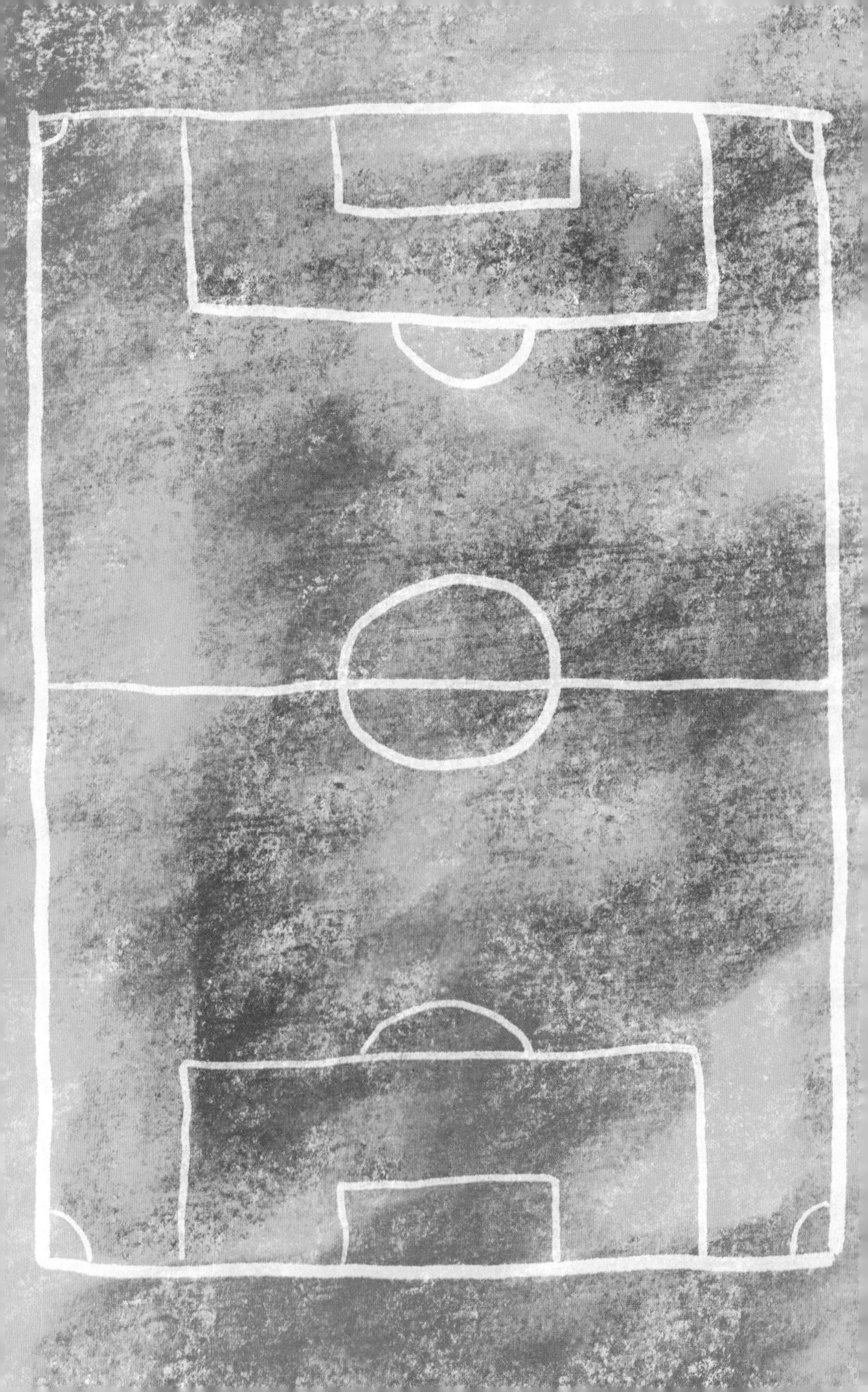

Red keeper,
ready?

Gold keeper,
ready?

CHAPTER 1

The Creation of the Girls

Everyone knows how birds are created.

girds

Less is known about how birds become girls.

Our flock came from the banks of the Ohio River.

As with all girls, our wings were removed.

But we were given special gifts that few girls had before,

and we had to learn how to use them.

Mr. Ryan's video begins with a still shot, one of dozens of team photos we'll take over the years.

Our uniforms have sashes like we're all Miss America.

I'm in the middle in blue — the keeper.

Our team was the 1971 Cardinals, named for Ohio's state bird and the year we were all born.

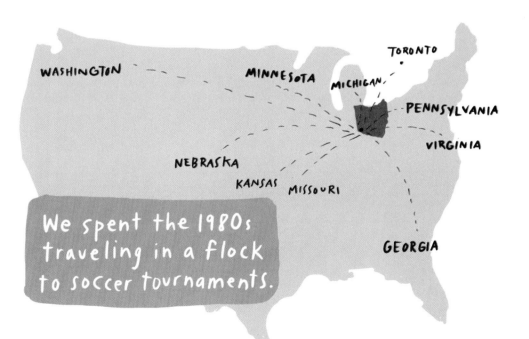

We spent the 1980s traveling in a flock to soccer tournaments.

A flock of CARDINALS

is called

a RADIANCE.

And we were radiant.

Every tournament we touched
turned to gold.

Mr. Ryan,
a cyborg in cutoff
jeans, recorded
it all.

(Sally's dad)

In 1987, we competed in the U.S. Girls' Nationals tournament in Seattle.

I was 16.

(My hair suffered from a combination of hairspray & Sun In.)

Seattle was as far from Ohio

as I'd ever been.

The top 4 teams in the country were there:
California, Texas, New York, and us—Ohio.

Everything was fancy.

My teammates and I felt important because people other than Mr. Ryan filmed our games and interviewed us, two at a time.

Not one of us said:

are these the same

questions

you ask

the boys' teams?

Maybe the questions weren't so far off.

One of my teammates got pregnant the next year.

And another the year after that.

I was about to start dating the guy I would eventually marry.

(And divorce.)

Most of us became

teachers,

nurses,

Stay-at-home
moms.

It makes me wonder: Can different QUESTIONS conjure different FUTURES?

But in 1987,

there was no
Women's World Cup.

No women's soccer
in the Olympics.

We'd never heard of a
U.S. Women's National Team.

We STILL haven't had a woman president.

I have photos and
fuzzy memories of
those times.

Now, all these
years later, I have
Mr. Ryan's video.

And my soccer days are given back to me:
refracted, animated, edited.

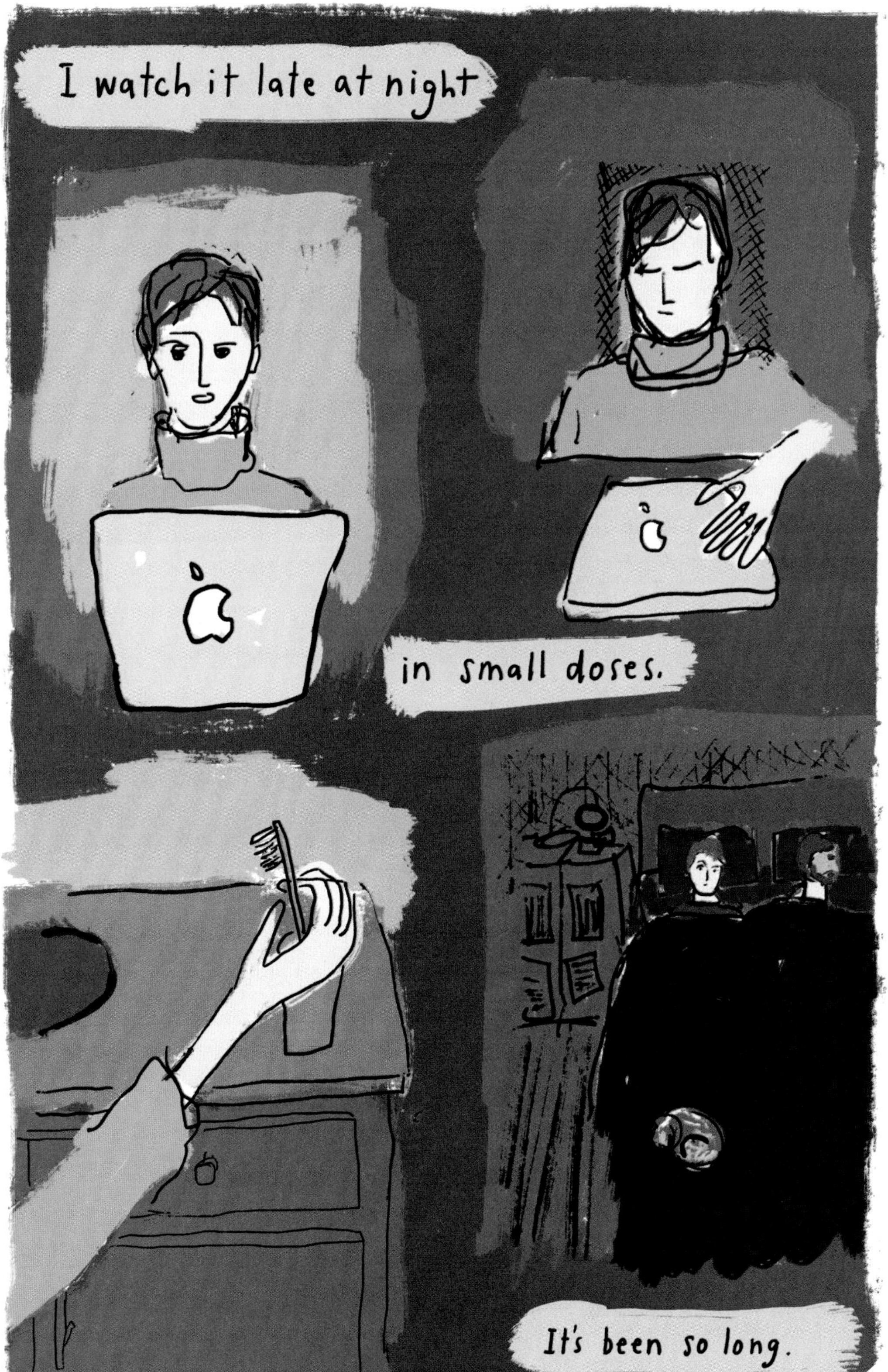
I watch it late at night
in small doses.
It's been so long.

We came in third in the tournament, which was a disappointment.

We weren't used to losing.

The man who spoke at the banquet was right. Mostly.

I never forgot that we were the third best team in the country that year. But I forgot so many other things.

I forgot him entirely.

I forgot the flowers and the Pepsi cans.

I forgot that our coach Mrs. Lynn talked about being...

...the only woman in a man's organization...

while a dad in a Cardinal costume looked on.

I forgot what it was like in the moments before a game, when the team was the only thing that mattered.

And what it was like to move through the world as a team

with our parents never far away.

But now, with Mr. Ryan's video,
I can see it all.

CHAPTER
2

The Palmist

Like all goalkeepers,
I had a magical power.

My HANDS.

This would require
special training.

(My roommate and me at
OVERNIGHT goalie camp.)

One of the first things we learned at camp was the importance of the "W."

Without it —

Formed by touching the tips of both thumbs, the W creates a barrier that stops the ball.

the ball can slip through your hands

and into your face.

Or worse: the back of the net.

I learned to use geometry to cut down scoring angles.

How to use the heel of my hand to lift the ball over the crossbar

and the flat top of my fist for a powerful punch.

↑ tuck in elbow so you don't pop out shoulder on a dive

I learned to use my body to protect my body.

← bend knee and flex foot for power and protection

Decades later, I would realize I received more preparation to be a KEEPER than I did to become a MOTHER.

At goalie camp
they told us to
practice at home.

Soft hands, they said.
Lots of reps.
Remember the **W**.

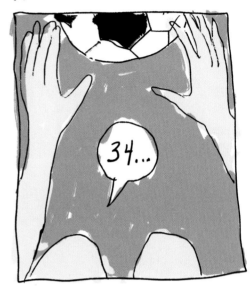

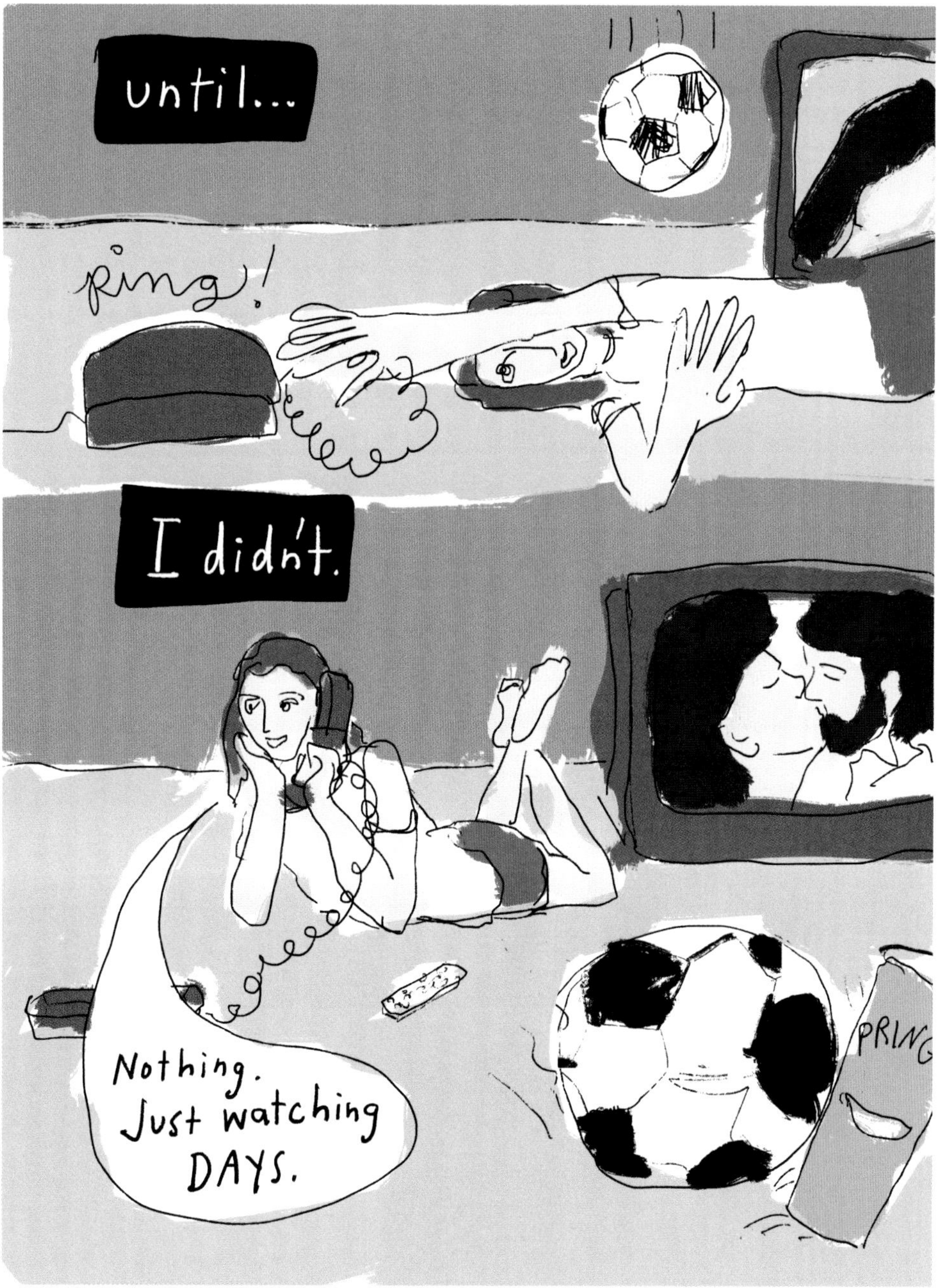
until...
ring!
I didn't.
Nothing. Just watching DAYS.
PRING

I became a keeper by accident.

I was 12 years old, the new girl, and I showed up at the wrong tryouts. The wrong team told me I was in the wrong position. I'd make their team (the better team) if I would be their goalkeeper.

"To be put in goal is to be punished," says James Irwin. "The position of goalkeeper is reserved for... the lazy, and the talentless."

Okay.

I probably wouldn't have chosen to be a keeper.

But I can't think of a position more suited to me.

In his article, Irwin admits he loved being a goalie. And he argues that there is a connection between ⟶

"being a writer and being a goalkeeper."

"It is a very individual position— the loneliest, most isolated role on the pitch."

"There are only a handful of well-known writers who've played competitive football. And every one of them played as a goalkeeper."

Every one of them was also a MAN.

Two of the best-known
writers who were goalkeepers are:

ALBERT
Camus and Nabokov
VLADIMIR

All that I
know most surely
about morality
and obligations,
I owe to football.

Camus ↑

I was crazy about
goalkeeping. That gallant art
had always been surrounded
with a halo of
singular glamour.

Nabokov

Like Nabokov and Camus,
I was a goalkeeper who wanted
to be a writer.

Unlike them,

I was a girl.

Humans have played a form of football for...

ever.

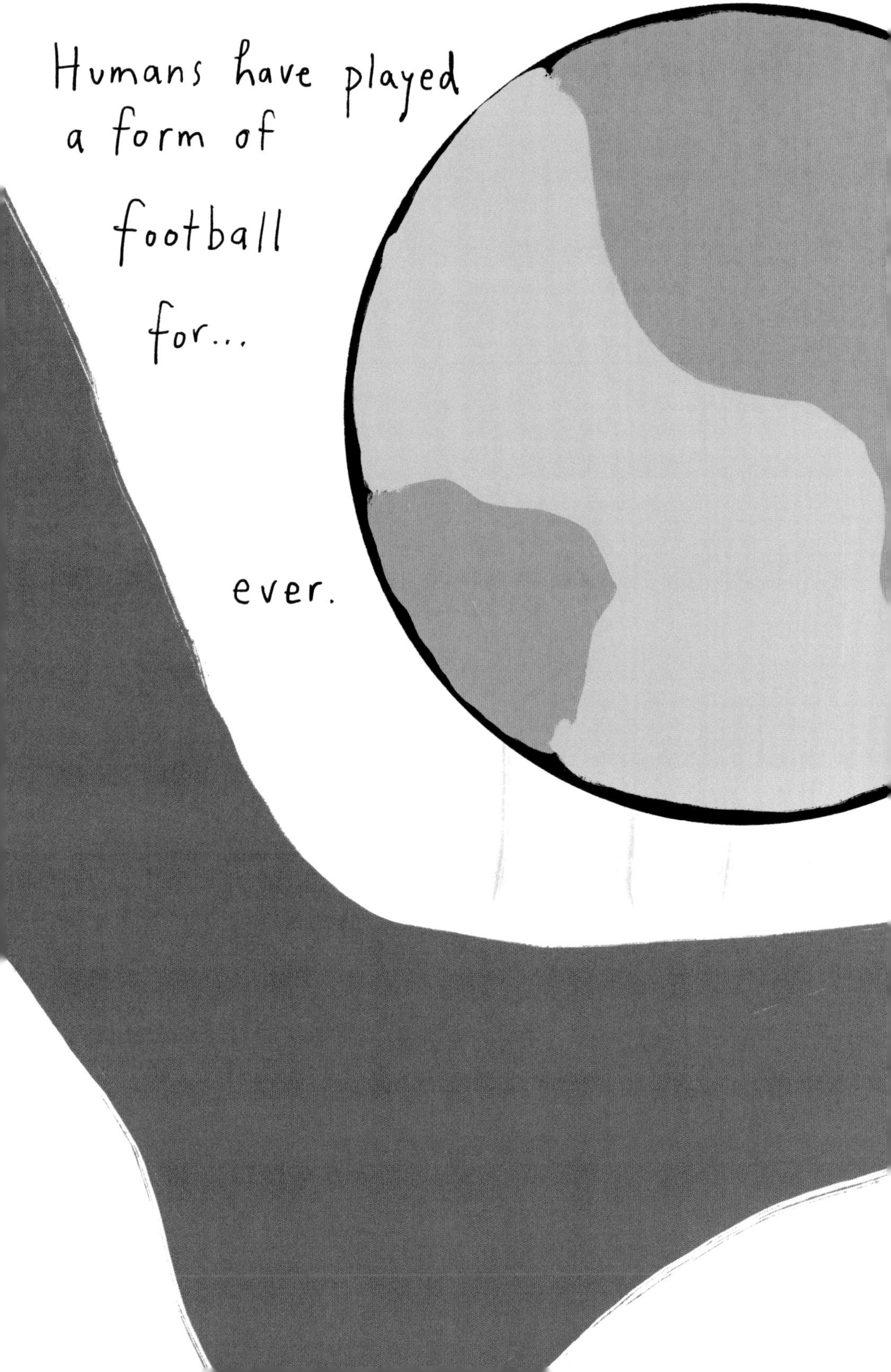

The Chinese played it.

The Ancient Greeks.

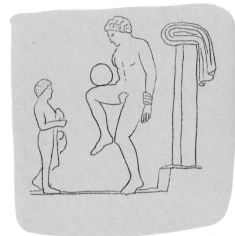

The Aztecs.

Medieval knights.

Shakespeare referenced it.

You base football player!

from KING LEAR

Native American men <u>and</u> women played it.

But it wasn't until 1871 that the
GOALKEEPER
became an official position.

Nabokov loved the
mystique of the keeper.

He is the lone eagle,
the man of mystery,
the last defender.

Not everyone shared his enthusiasm.

The striker
sparks delight and
the goalkeeper,
a wet blanket,
snuffs it out.

Eduardo Galeano,
SOCCER IN SUN AND SHADOW

Women's soccer as we know it began in 1881 as *Ladies' Football*

and it began with a goalkeeper.

Helen Matthews was a Scottish suffragist who organized the first public matches between Scotland and England.

CATTLE MARKET INN ATHLETIC GROUNDS, STANLEY, LIVERPOOL.
RETURN VISIT OF THE INTERNATIONAL
LADY FOOTBALL PLAYERS.
ENGLAND V. SCOTLAND.
TWO GRAND MATCHES.
THIS DAY (SATURDAY) AND MONDAY NEXT,
THE 25TH AND 27TH INSTANT.
Kick-off—Saturday at Five p.m.; Monday at 7 30 p.m.
ADMISSION, ONE SHILLING.

She gave herself the pseudonym
MRS. GRAHAM.

How did she know to conceal her identity?

Had she learned from her suffrage work to expect violence when women challenge the status quo?

The players had a troubling reception in the papers and on the pitch. They faced condescension, mockery, critiques of their play and clothing, bawdy jeers, and mob violence.

↖ Nicholas Lane Jackson was a sports journalist and assistant secretary of the Football Association.

DISORDERLY SCENE
AT A WOMEN'S FOOTBALL MATCH

vulgar curiosity

what is termed a "ladies'" football match

a costume which is neither graceful
nor very becoming

a crowd of youths

boisterous

Play—if kicking the ball about the field
can be so described

a great multitude

a large number

police constables

so-called match

a great rush

possession

the mob

rough treatment

the women

the clamour

the rush

the jeers

much disorder

the players

driven away

THE MANCHESTER GUARDIAN, JUNE 22, 1881

After just 2 months, play ended.

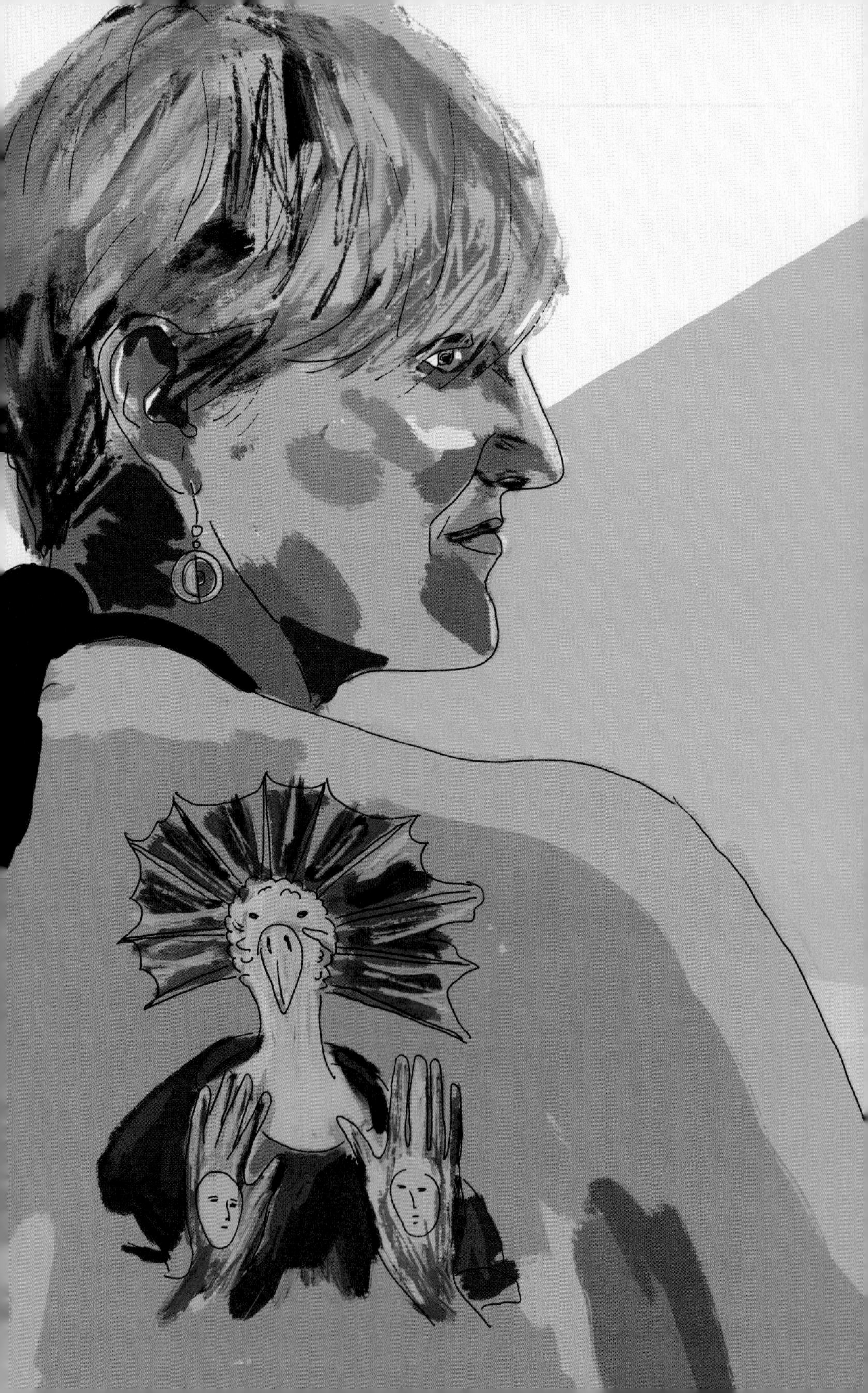

In my early goalie days,
I was still 30 years
away from getting a tattoo

of *Leonora*

Carrington's

sculpture THE PALMIST,

with its magical hands.

It reminds me of
the power of women and art.

These days I'm a writer and professor,
and my life is quiet, focused on
books, art, and teaching.

It's easy to feel far away
from that girl on the soccer field.

But looking back now I wonder:

If I could have looked into my teenaged GOALKEEPER palms,

What would I have seen
in my FUTURE?

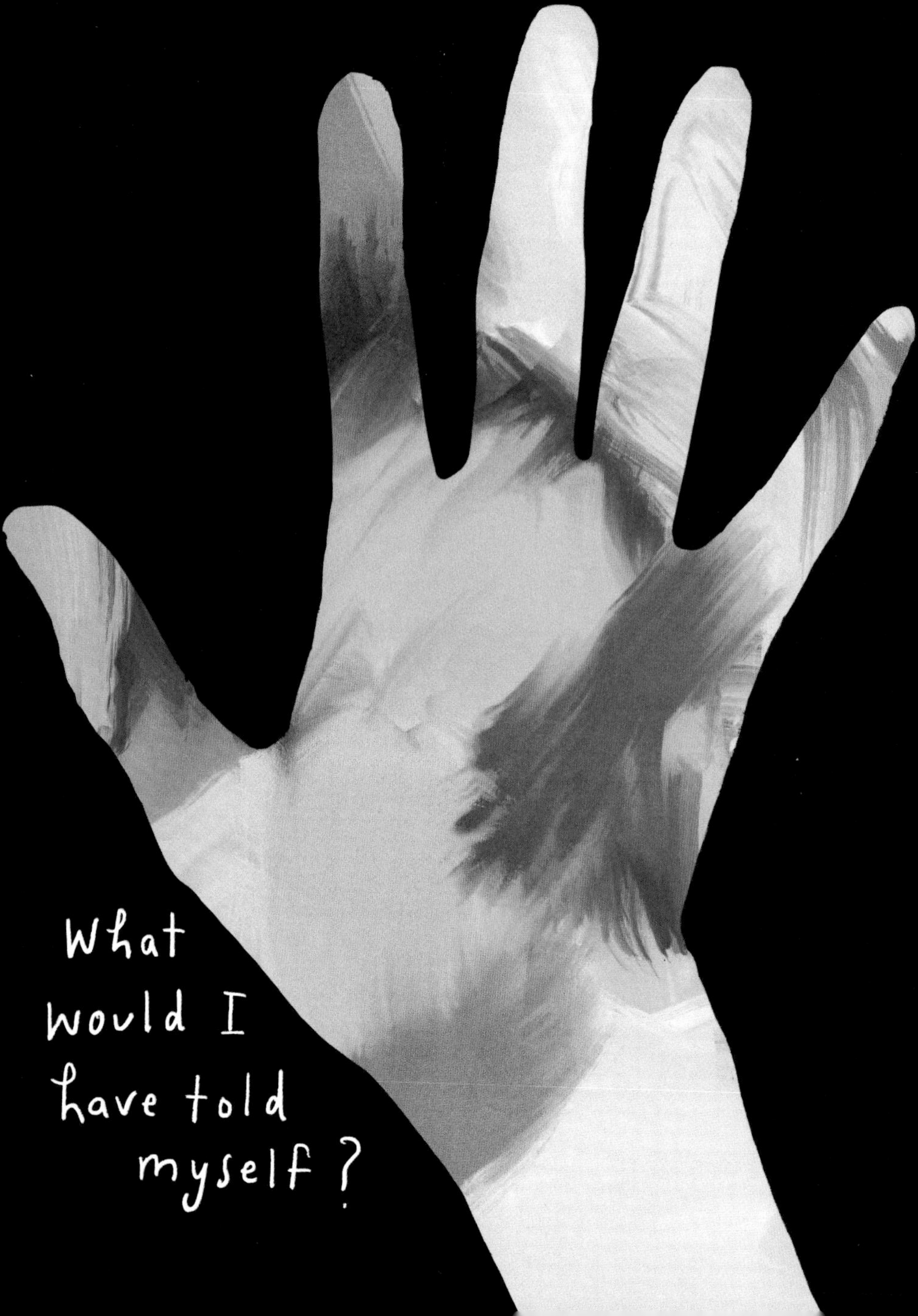

What
would I
have told
myself?

CHAPTER

3

A Boy's Life

Growing up, I had a boy's life.

Or at least that's how I think of it now.

I was the first one* picked for gym teams.

I could throw a perfect spiral.

I kicked
Home Runs in
cul-de-sac
kickball.

Here I am
on the cover
of our local
magazine
playing soccer
with boys.

But occasionally I would be reminded that I was, in fact,

a girl.

And that there were differences between being a boy and being a girl.

When I started school, I was given a keepsake book to record my activities and store mementos.

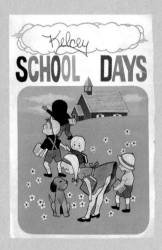

I learned that one difference between boys and girls is that girls get depicted bending over with their bloomers showing.

Another difference is what boys and girls get to be when they grow up.

Each year the SCHOOL DAYS book asked me to choose.

At first, I didn't distinguish between boys' and girls' careers. →

FIRST GRADE

WHEN I GROW UP I WANT TO BE:

BOYS
- [ ] ASTRONAUT
- [ ] FOOTBALL PLAYER
- [✓] BASEBALL PLAYER
- [ ] HOCKEY PLAYER
- [ ] CHEF
- [ ] FIREMAN
- [✓] POLICEMAN
- [ ] SOLDIER
- [ ] COWBOY
- [ ] ARTIST

GIRLS
- [✓] MOTHER
- [ ] NURSE
- [ ] TEACHER
- [ ] ACTRESS
- [ ] SINGER
- [ ] MODEL
- [ ] SECRETARY
- [ ] BIOLOGIST
- [ ] ARTIST
- [ ] AIR HOSTESS

OTHER _____

SECOND GRADE

WHEN I GROW UP I WANT TO BE:

BOYS
- [ ] ASTRONAUT
- [✓] FOOTBALL PLAYER
- [✓] BASEBALL PLAYER
- [ ] HOCKEY PLAYER
- [ ] CHEF
- [ ] FIREMAN
- [✓] POLICEMAN
- [ ] SOLDIER
- [ ] COWBOY
- [ ] ARTIST

GIRLS
- [ ] MOTHER
- [ ] NURSE
- [✓] TEACHER
- [ ] ACTRESS
- [ ] SINGER
- [ ] MODEL
- [✓] SECRETARY
- [ ] BIOLOGIST
- [✓] ARTIST
- [ ] AIR HOSTESS

OTHER _____ Soccer _____

In 2nd grade, I even added an "other" that would surely have belonged on the boys' side. ↙

Why did a 2nd-grade girl in the 1970s check so many SPORTS?

51

When I was born, my dad was still in college, where he'd just finished his final season of Division I football.

He'd hoped for a boy.

Baby me with Dad at his graduation

And he raised me like a boy. He taught me to throw a football, hit a baseball, and shoot a basketball.

In kindergarten I got the best gift: a NY Giants uniform with full pads. I felt so powerful in it.

My parents signed me up for soccer when I was in 1st grade. My mom still recalls my dad cheering me on.

Atta girl! Draw blood!

There weren't any girls' teams then, so I played on co-ed teams, and my dad bought a book to learn the game and became our coach.

I was tall and strong, as good as the boys. But by 3rd grade, it seems, I had learned that I was a girl—

THIRD GRADE

WHEN I GROW UP I WANT TO BE:

BOYS		GIRLS	
☐ ASTRONAUT	☐ FIREMAN	☑ MOTHER	☐ MODEL
☐ FOOTBALL PLAYER	☐ POLICEMAN	☐ NURSE	☐ SECRETARY
☐ BASEBALL PLAYER	☐ SOLDIER	☑ TEACHER	☐ BIOLOGIST
☐ HOCKEY PLAYER	☐ COWBOY	☑ ACTRESS	☑ ARTIST
☐ CHEF	☐ ARTIST	☐ SINGER	☐ AIR HOSTESS

OTHER *Soccer Player*

and to limit my choices accordingly.

The only thing both boys and girls could be was ARTIST.

FOURTH GRADE

WHEN I GROW UP I WANT TO BE:

BOYS		GIRLS	
☐ ASTRONAUT	☐ FIREMAN	☑ MOTHER	☐ MODEL
☐ FOOTBALL PLAYER	☐ POLICEMAN	☐ NURSE	☐ SECRETARY
☐ BASEBALL PLAYER	☐ SOLDIER	☐ TEACHER	☑ BIOLOGIST
☐ HOCKEY PLAYER	☐ COWBOY	☐ ACTRESS	☑ ARTIST
☐ CHEF	☐ ARTIST	☐ SINGER	☐ AIR HOSTESS

OTHER ____SOCCER____

In 2nd, 3rd, and 4th grades, I wanted to be an artist. (A girl artist.) I wonder what I thought that meant?

I didn't know any artists the way I knew mothers, teachers, and secretaries. I just knew I liked to draw.

In 4th and 5th grades, I also wanted to be a biologist.

I'd been given a butterfly-collecting kit.

My preferred quarry was tiger swallowtails, abundant in my Pennsylvania yard.

I didn't know that young Vladimir Nabokov had been a lepidopterist.

In his memoir, SPEAK, MEMORY, Nabokov describes a swallowtail as:

"a splendid pale-yellow creature with black blotches, blue crenels,

and a cinnabar eyespot above each chrome-rimmed black tail."

Perhaps what most appealed to me was their resemblance to the black-and-gold uniforms of the Pittsburgh Pirates and Steelers in what was, in the late 1970s, the City of Champions.

Like many sporty girls, my heroes were usually male athletes.

Oh how I wanted to be like

Lynn Swann,

the graceful and gravity-defying wide receiver for the Steelers.

As if his name wasn't elegant enough, he was also a

ballet dancer.

In 4th grade, I wrote and scratched out "SOCCER." In 5th grade, I did the same with "ATHLETE." ——→

FIFTH GRADE

WHEN I GROW UP I WANT TO BE:

BOYS
- [ ] ASTRONAUT
- [ ] FOOTBALL PLAYER
- [ ] BASEBALL PLAYER
- [ ] HOCKEY PLAYER
- [ ] CHEF
- [ ] FIREMAN
- [ ] POLICEMAN
- [ ] SOLDIER
- [ ] COWBOY
- [ ] ARTIST

GIRLS
- [ ] MOTHER
- [ ] NURSE
- [ ] TEACHER
- [ ] ACTRESS
- [ ] SINGER
- [ ] MODEL
- [ ] SECRETARY
- [x] BIOLOGIST
- [ ] ARTIST
- [ ] AIR HOSTESS

OTHER ~~Athlete~~

I think of what Virginia Woolf said of her sister, Vanessa Bell:
"Once I saw her scrawl on a black door...

VANESSA BELL

...WHEN I AM A FAMOUS PAINTER...

and then turned shy and rubbed it out."

57

Why did she write and then erase her dreams?
Why did I? Did I too "turn shy"? (I was
a shy kid.) Did I look around and notice
that there were no grown-up women
soccer players?

Those of us who were not
fantasizing about a white
wedding or the man of
our dreams knew we
were freaks.

We knew better than
to speak our longings.

bell
hooks

Or had I already
learned—as I'd learned
to keep my dreams
on the GIRLS' side—

not to SPEAK MY LONGINGS?

But bell hooks was born in the 1950s.
I was born in the 1970s.

Weren't things different?

While I recall wanting to be a football or baseball player, I have no recollection of wanting to be a "POLICEMAN," which I checked off in 1st and 2nd grades.

There can only be one explanation.

CHARLIE'S ANGELS debuted in 1976, and my sister and I watched every episode, collected trading cards, and "played" Charlie's Angels.

We had matching water guns shaped like the ones the Angels used.

We raided our mom's purse collection to conceal our weapons in style.

And we patrolled the house in search of

BAD GUYS.

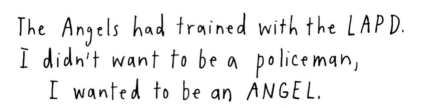

The Angels had trained with the LAPD. I didn't want to be a policeman, I wanted to be an ANGEL.

The point is, things were changing.
Girls were seeing:

STRONG WOMEN

HOLD IT RIGHT THERE, CREEP.

SMART WOMEN

WORKING WOMEN

I can bring home the bacon, fry it up in a pan.

The feminist movement had caused a shift.

But, as the saying goes, the more things change,

ONE FOR THE ANGELS!

And never never never let you forget you're a MAN.

↑ Enjoli perfume ad

the more they stay the same.

Maybe it's no surprise that by 6th grade, there was only one thing I wanted to be when I grew up.

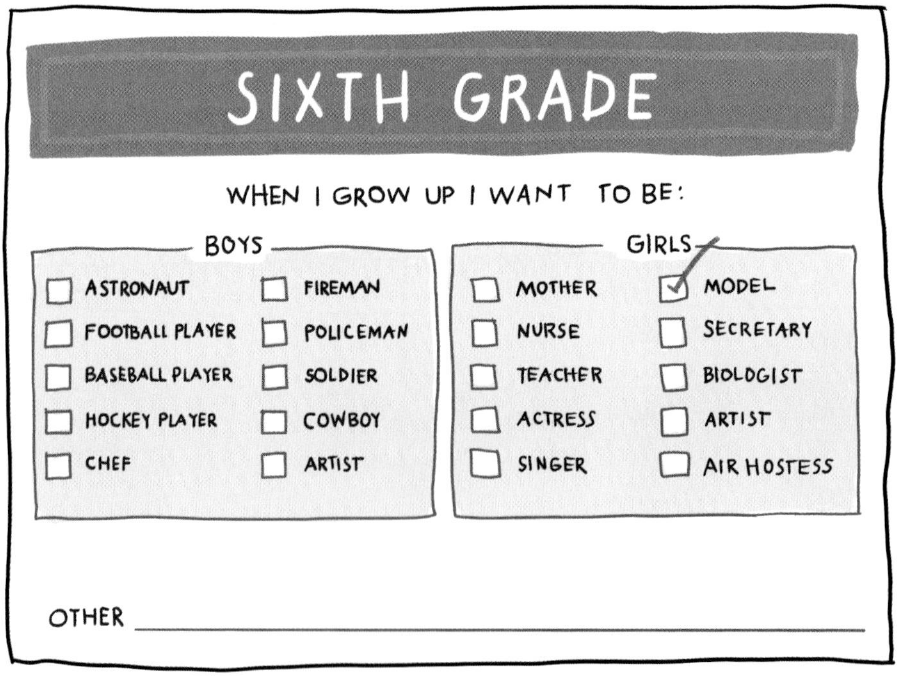
SIXTH GRADE
WHEN I GROW UP I WANT TO BE:
BOYS
ASTRONAUT
FOOTBALL PLAYER
BASEBALL PLAYER
HOCKEY PLAYER
CHEF
FIREMAN
POLICEMAN
SOLDIER
COWBOY
ARTIST
GIRLS
MOTHER
NURSE
TEACHER
ACTRESS
SINGER
MODEL
SECRETARY
BIOLOGIST
ARTIST
AIR HOSTESS
OTHER

CHAPTER 4

The Basis of Sex

Sixth grade is when I moved to Cincinnati and became the goalkeeper for the Cardinals. It was 1983, the year my teammates and I all turned 12.

Lolita's age.

VLADIMIR NABOKOV
"The only convincing love story of our century" —Vanity Fair
Lolita
"my hot downy darling"
"her lips as red as licked red candy"
"and the seaside of her schoolgirl thighs"

We hadn't read LOLITA and didn't know that Cincinnati's public library had been the first to ban it.

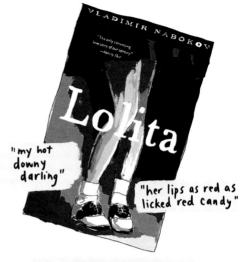

But we knew that Miss OHIO had recently become Miss AMERICA.

And that MADONNA was nothing like a virgin.

madonna
like a virgin
BOY TOY

We passed the time at tournaments by choreographing a dance to the PRINCE song "D.M.S.R.," which we performed... for our parents?

DANCE
MUSIC
SEX
ROMANCE

Girl, it aint no use / you might as well get loose / work your body like a whore

This is just the sort of memory I'd think I must have made up. Dancing to a smutty PRINCE song? In front of our parents?
But there it is in Mr. Ryan's video, minute 48.

At the end of each game, we lined up to touch hands and trade team patches.

And utter the low, trochaic chant:

Our mothers sewed the patches onto our jackets.

We felt so cool in our CARDINALS jackets.

Like a 1980s version of the PINK LADIES.

I suffered my first kiss when a boy put mine on at the end of a basketball game.

C'mon, give it back. My mom's waiting for me.

I'll give it back if you give me a KISS.

I never let another boy wear it.

My mom has kept my jacket all these years.

Hey Mom! Can you find my old Cardinals jacket and text me a pic?

For literature!

CARDINALS

The next time I visit her in Cincinnati, she says:

I've got a whole box of Cardinals stuff. Do you want it?

HOW I PICTURE THE BOX:

HOW IT ACTUALLY LOOKS:

Office Depot
Copy paper

CARDINALS

But it is a TREASURE. I learn, for example, that my mother was the team's PRESS CORRESPONDENT.

I see her articles progress from cursive notes

The 1971 Girls Southea Cincinnati select soccer successfully defended

FOR IMMEDIATE '71 CARDINALS WIN

FOR IMMEDIATE RELEASE
'71 CARDS WIN BAY CHALLENGE CUP

'71 Cards win Bay Challenge Cup

to hand-lettered drafts

to typed press releases

to published newspaper clippings.

She kept it ALL. Meeting agendas, travel itineraries, notes on fundraisers. Items that I as a parent years later would throw away as soon as possible.

At the time, I never gave any thought to all the work our parents did.

Or to the fact they were living their own lives too.

I got a harsh reminder when my parents got divorced.

My handsome dad watching a scary movie with us at a tournament hotel.

Sports remained a constant amid the upheaval of moving from one house into two different houses, of my parents dating new people.

I could put on my uniform or practice equipment and become someone else with a focus, a mission.

In our uniforms, my teammates and I were no longer even GIRLS, we were PLAYERS, we were ATHLETES.

Everywhere else we were told to

BE GOOD

BE QUIET

and

and

BE NICE.

But on the soccer field
we were free to

BE TOUGH

BE AGGRESSIVE

and

BE POWERFUL

As a keeper I dreamed of making the flashy and dramatic save. And sometimes I did. But it was just as fun when the goal box was crowded and chaotic —

and the ball appeared in my magical hands.

and I'd look down and the ball would be in my hand," said Ervick. "I didn't know how it got there."

(CINCINNATI ENQUIRER)

Mr. Ryan's video includes multiple post-tournament trophy ceremonies.

Woohoo!

Way to go, Kelcey!

Even now I feel both embarrassed and pleased by the extra cheers I often received as keeper.

It all felt new and exciting.

It felt like we were doing
something that

GIRLS HADN'T DONE BEFORE.

We knew our moms hadn't done it. Our moms were the

ORIGINAL SOCCER MOMS

(A decade before anyone heard the term.)

They taught us to make hair accessories in our team colors.

Performed cheerleading routines for us before games,

(Mr. Ryan's video, minute 32.)

Drove us to practice in station wagons.
(No minivans yet.)

And raised travel money by printing and selling a recipe book.

(We still make Mrs. Schmidt's Cheesy Sausage Breakfast Casserole.)

We knew our moms hadn't grown up playing competitive sports, but we didn't know 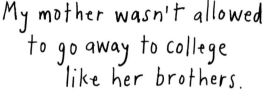 WHY.

We didn't know that, when our mothers gave birth to us in 1971, fewer than 300,000 girls played high school sports compared to 3,000,000 boys.

We didn't know that in 1971 our mothers couldn't get a credit card without a man to co-sign.

My mother wasn't allowed to go away to college like her brothers.

Instead she married my dad and worked odd jobs while he finished college.

She lost those jobs as soon as her pregnancy started showing.

She was 21 years old.

← me

We definitely didn't know that in 1971, nearly 50 years since the Equal Rights Amendment had been introduced, a new group would attempt to pass it.

Dr. Bernice Sandler was on the front lines.

She had just gotten her doctorate but was not considered for any of the 7 jobs open in her department.

She asked a male colleague WHY.

"Let's face it," he said, "you come on too strong for a woman."
I DID NOT KNOW... THOSE WORDS WOULD CHANGE MY LIFE... [AND] THE LIVES OF MILLIONS OF WOMEN AND GIRLS BECAUSE THEY WOULD ULTIMATELY LEAD TO TITLE IX.
INSTEAD I WENT HOME AND CRIED.
sandler
(I am a crier, and it gives me great satisfaction to know that Title IX started with a woman's tears.)

WHENEVER THINGS GO WRONG IN MY LIFE, I START TO READ ABOUT THE PROBLEM.

I AM A GREAT BELIEVER IN

BIBLIOTHERAPY.

(I am also a reader and English professor, so I am equally pleased that TITLE IX began with a woman reading.)

Sandler researched the Civil Rights Act of 1964, where so much foundational work had been done. She came across a "little-known Presidential Executive Order" prohibiting discrimination by federal contractors, which she knew would apply to universities. It did not include sex discrimination, but there was a FOOTNOTE.

AND BEING AN ACADEMIC, I READ FOOTNOTES.

The footnote said that the order had recently been amended to include _sex discrimination._

I ACTUALLY SHRIEKED ALOUD.

The discovery led her to file a class-action sex-discrimination lawsuit against: 250 COLLEGES AND UNIVERSITIES in the U.S.

I'M THE CHAIR OF THE SUBCOMMITTEE ON HIGHER EDUCATION.

LET'S HOLD SOME HEARINGS ON THIS!

EDITH GREEN
Democrat for
CONGRESS

I'LL TESTIFY!

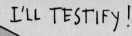

In her testimony Rep. Shirley Chisholm claimed:

Gentlemen, you know that I get discriminated against all the time for being Black. But that's nothing compared to how much I get for being a woman.

Rep. PATSY MINK
joined the cause.

Patsy Mink was the first woman of color
elected to Congress. She'd wanted to be
a doctor but was denied entry to medical
schools because she was a woman.
She wanted to be a lawyer but couldn't get
a job because of her interracial marriage.

BECAUSE THERE WERE ONLY 8 WOMEN
WHO WERE MEMBERS OF CONGRESS,
I ALWAYS FELT THAT WE WERE
SERVING A DUAL ROLE...
REPRESENTING OUR OWN
DISTRICTS AND... HAVING
TO VOICE THE CONCERNS
OF THE TOTAL
POPULATION OF
WOMEN.

And they got an ally in the Senate, Birch Bayh of Indiana.

WE HAD BEEN TRYING TO BRING THE EQUAL RIGHTS AMENDMENT AND FEARED THAT EVEN AFTER PASSAGE IT COULD TAKE YEARS BEFORE THE STATES RATIFIED.

MY WIFE MARVELLA EDUCATED ME ABOUT DISCRIMINATION AGAINST WOMEN IN HIGHER EDUCATION AFTER BEING TOLD BY THE UNIVERSITY OF VIRGINIA THAT...

VIRGINIA

Women need not apply.

85

Armed with 1,200 pages of evidence of sex discrimination compiled by Dr. Sandler, but concerned that the ERA might be a NO, they pushed for something "smaller": the 37 words of

TITLE IX OF THE
EDUCATION AMENDMENTS ACT
OF 1972.

NO PERSON IN THE UNITED STATES SHALL,
ON THE BASIS OF SEX,
BE EXCLUDED FROM PARTICIPATION IN,
BE DENIED THE BENEFITS OF,
OR
BE SUBJECTED TO DISCRIMINATION UNDER
ANY EDUCATION PROGRAM OR ACTIVITY
RECEIVING FEDERAL FINANCIAL ASSISTANCE.

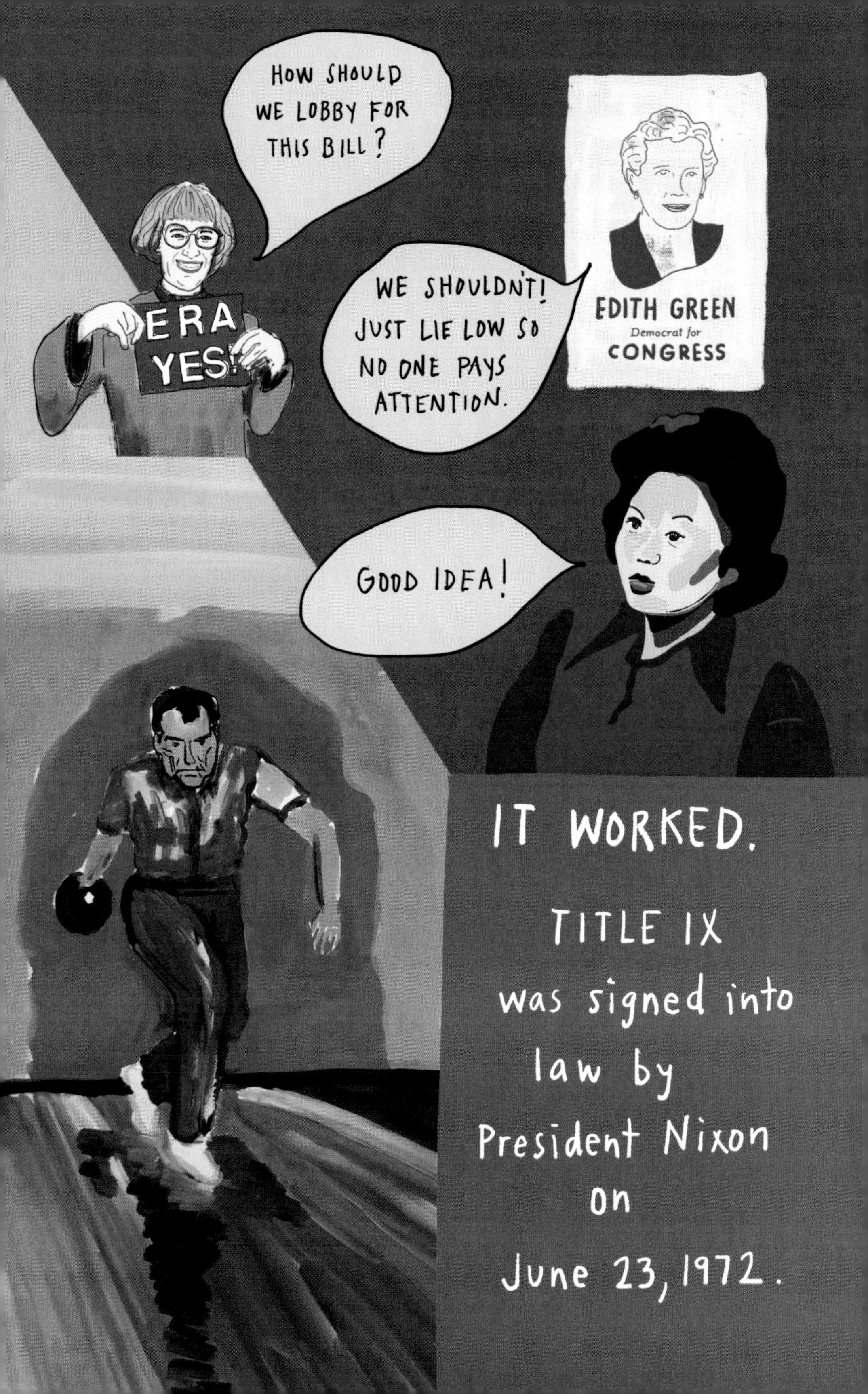

HOW SHOULD WE LOBBY FOR THIS BILL?
ERA YES!
EDITH GREEN
Democrat for
CONGRESS
WE SHOULDN'T! JUST LIE LOW SO NO ONE PAYS ATTENTION.
GOOD IDEA!
IT WORKED.
TITLE IX
was signed into
law by
President Nixon
on
June 23, 1972.

No one seemed to know what the implications would be.

But Title IX
would change
everything.

GOD
BLESS YOU,
**TITLE
IX**

Sandler

"Title IX
can claim
World Cups
and Olympic
gold medals
as part of
its legacy."

Since Title IX,
"female [athletic]
participation has
exploded — by
1063%."

Source:
MS. MAGAZINE

Number of
girls in high
school sports:
1971 / 293,000
vs
2019 / 3,400,000

My teammates and I
didn't know any of this.

But it shaped our
entire lives.

CHAPTER 5

Rough Girls

In 1895, fourteen years after "Mrs. Graham" set up a series of women's matches, a player who called herself NETTIE J. HONEYBALL established the BRITISH LADIES' FOOTBALL CLUB and took out an ad for the first match.

THE British Ladies' Football

President—LADY FLORENCE DIX

THE FIRST LADIES
FOOTBALL MATC
(NORTH V. SOUTH)

WILL BE PLAYED ON

urday, 23rd March, 189

UPON THE

UCH END ATHLETIC GROUND

NIGHTINGALE LANE, HORNSEY.

KICK OFF 4.30.

e Ladies' Match will be preceded by

CROUCH END V. 3rd GRENADIER GUARDS,

KICK OFF 3 O'CLOCK.

Admission (including both Matches) 1s.

Covered Stand, 1s. extra.

Frequent Trains from Moorgate Street, Broad Street, King's Cross, and intermediate stations to Hornsey.

Ladies desirous of joining the above Club should apply to Miss NETTIE J. HONEYBALL, "Ellesmere," 27, Weston Park, Crouch End, N.

Footballs by COOK.   Caps by A. E. RAISIN, of Stroud Green Road.

W. & W. J. Mizen, Printers, 13, Stroud Green Road, N.

Before that first match was played, the press made clear what it expected of lady footballers, and what lady footballers could expect from the press: mockery, condescension, and an obsession with their bodies.

It was the era of the NEW WOMAN, who was challenging traditional gender roles and Victorian ideas of womanhood— AND manhood.

ARRIVING

THE POOR REFEREE

OH BOTHER THE RULES

HALF TIME

THE GOOD LOOKING GOALKEEPER

THE FOOTBALL EDITION

Nettie Honeyball partnered with
LADY FLORENCE DIXIE,
who served as the first president of the new
British Ladies' Football Club.

There is no reason why football should not be played by women... provided they dress RATIONALLY and relegate to limbo the straightjacket attire which fashion delights to attire them.

Lady Dixie was a proponent of RATIONAL DRESS, which is exactly what it sounds like: a push for women to wear clothing that makes sense and doesn't deform the body.

She viewed football as a way to promote this feminist issue.

TO
ALL WOMEN
AND
HONOURABLE, UPRIGHT, AND COURAGEOUS
MEN

I dedicate the following pages, with the hope that a straightforward inspection of the evils afflicting Society, will lead to their demolition in the only way possible—namely, by giving to Women equal rights with Men.

Lady Dixie wasn't a footballer, she was a writer. In 1890 she published a novel about a feminist REVOLUTION.

In it, a young woman named Gloria de Lara pretends to be a man so she can join the House of Commons.

When her true identity is revealed, an army of women rise up to support her.

The revolution is triumphant, and Gloria becomes the first woman prime minister.

GLORIANA;

OR,

THE REVOLUTION OF 1900.

The first match in 1895 drew a crowd of 10,000, and an illustration of it appeared on the cover of THE GRAPHIC.

From its beginnings, "ladies' football" challenged notions of class, race, and gender.

Football was popular among working-class men, and here was a group of predominantly middle-class women on the pitch.

One of the players in that first match was Emma Clarke, now widely regarded as the first Black woman footballer in Britain.

Clarke lived a few streets away from "Mrs. Graham," who'd organized the matches 14 years earlier and was now widely praised as a goalkeeper.

"Mrs. Graham played a game which would not have disgraced many male exponents of goalkeeping."

But one player "completely diddled the BLUES goalkeeper [Mrs. Graham]" as well as the press's ideas about gender: a "laddish girl whose sex was certainly doubtful," called TOMMY.

The PALL MALL GAZETTE said "Tommy" was "built like a boy, ran like a boy, and seemed to know too much about the game for a girl of any size."

Actually, my name is Nellie.

The press justified its obsession with women's hips and chests from a biological perspective.

It must be clear to everybody that girls are totally unfitted for the ROUGH WORK of the football field.

A man charges with his chest and checks with his hips. Will doctors tell us these portions of a woman's body are fit for such ROUGH WORK?

THE SKETCH →
THE PALL MALL GAZETTE →

OSCAR WILDE addressed such debates rather cheekily.

Football is all very well as a game for ROUGH GIRLS, but it is hardly suitable for delicate boys.

Ladies' football continued to be treated like a farce. Nettie Honeyball defended the club.

There is nothing farcical about the BRITISH LADIES' FOOTBALL CLUB.

I founded the association late last year with the fixed resolve of proving to the world that women are not the "ornamental and useless" creatures men have pictured.

For her, for Lady Florence Dixie, for "Mrs. Graham," Nellie Gilbert ("Tommy"), Emma Clarke, and the rest of the players...

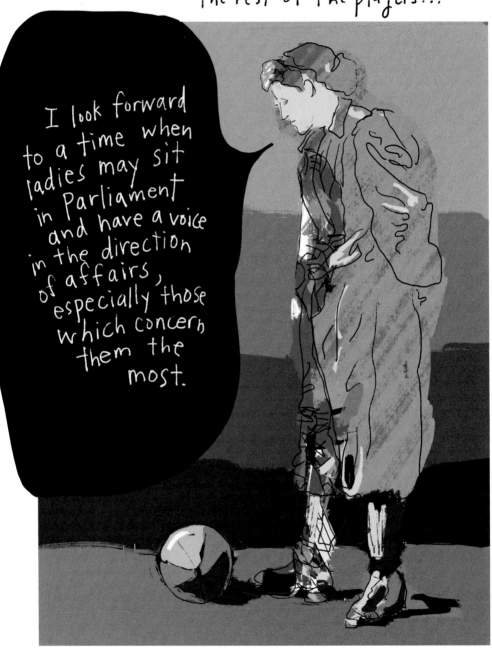

I look forward to a time when ladies may sit in Parliament and have a voice in the direction of affairs, especially those which concern them the most.

...it was always about so much more than football.

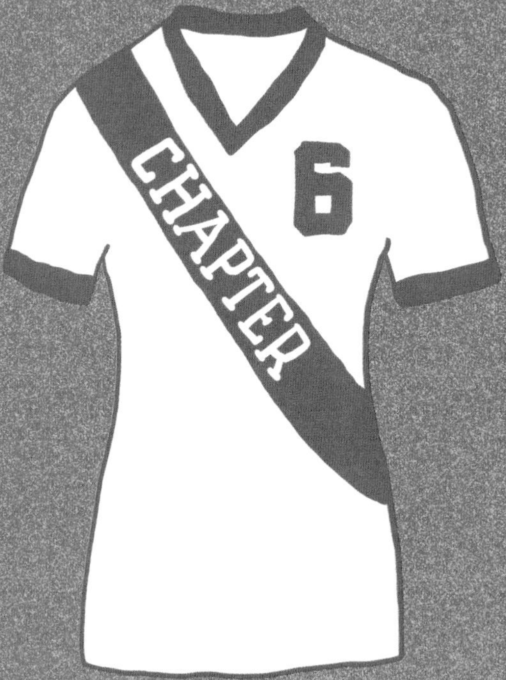
CHAPTER
6

Miss Ohio

In the Ohio River Valley, there are more hills than flatlands, and the flatlands that got turned into soccer fields were often flooded.

Barges the size of soccer fields floated down the river.

We practiced all year long near trees and train tracks, sometimes counting 100 train cars rumbling by. Mosquitoes. Mugginess.

There were layers of history in the land beneath our cleats: rumors of the Underground Railroad in the houses on the riverbanks, Native American names for land and water.

OHIO

Ohio River
from the Iroquois O-Y-O,
or Great River

KENTUCKY from the Iroquois
KEN-TAH-TEN,
or Land of Tomorrow

Mark Twain once said:

When the end of the world comes, I want to be in CINCINNATI because it's always 20 years behind the times.

CINCINNATI

We were on the east side of the city.

Twain was right about Cincinnati — with one exception.

Now I want to talk soccer, because Cincinnati is in the forefront of soccer cities anywhere in the U.S.

An example, the Cardinals, a group of young ladies from the east side of town who've won nearly 200 games in the span of 5 years.

DONN BURROWS 12

This group of 14-year-olds has conquered the state, and now the team will turn to the Midwest. Seven other states will compete for the Regional Championship in Overland Park, Kansas.

Mr. Ryan filmed the news crew filming our practice and interviewing our coaches.

Mr. Carter, my goalie coach who carpooled me to practice in his 5-speed BMW, gave his take on our success.

We have 18 girls of fairly comparable talent level. When we sub, we strengthen ourselves because the substitutes are just as strong and coming in fresh.

Mr. Grunwald
(Beth's dad)

Mrs. Lynn,
head coach
(Beth's mom)

(A different Beth)

(We had 3 Beths!)

(And 3 Amys!)

Mr. Grunwald, our soft-spoken
assistant coach, offered a different
perspective on our success.

We've pretty much
been TOGETHER.
We travel a lot.
We're always TOGETHER.
That's one of our big
things—we're a team,
we stay TOGETHER.

It was, and we were, and we did!

Our togetherness took many forms.

We're BIG, B-I-G and we're BAD, B-A-D
And we're BOSS, B-O-S, B-O-S-S, BOSS!
You may beat the others,
and you may beat the rest,
but you'll never beat the Cardinals
'Cause the Cardinals are the BEST!

We are the Cardinals, the mighty, mighty Cardinals,
Everywhere we go, people want to know
Who we are, what we do, so we tell them:
We are the Cardinals, the mighty, mighty Cardinals...

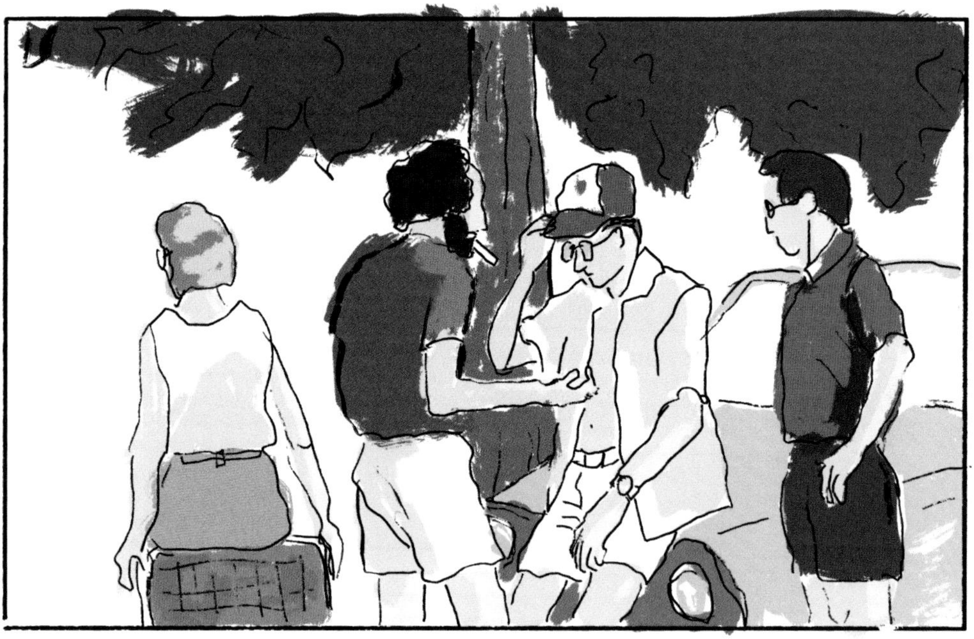

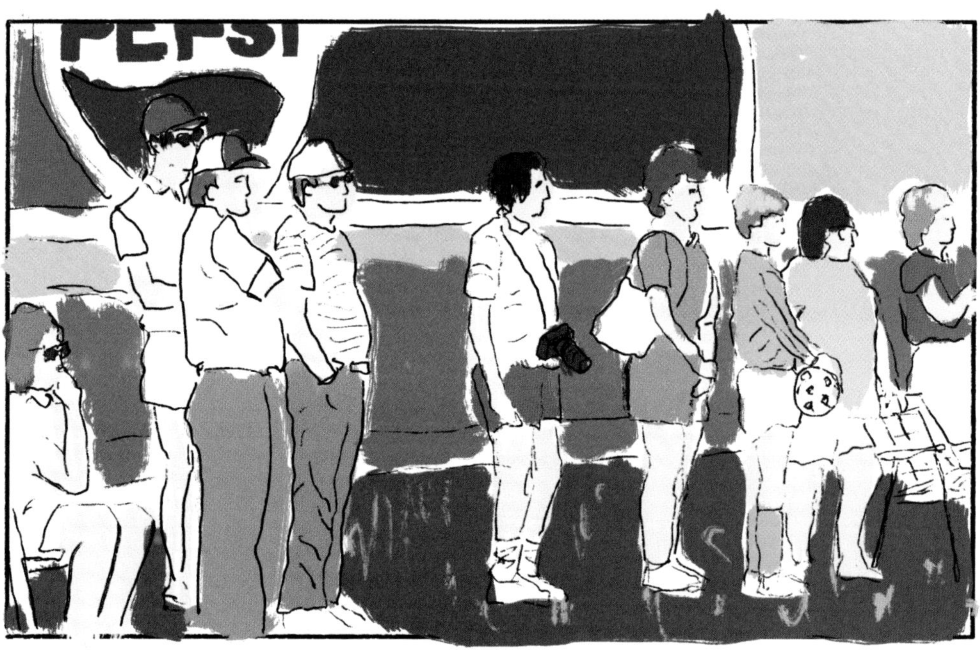

Little red Corvette, baby you're much too fast
Hating all the faking and shaking while I'm breaking your brittle heart...

♪ We're running...

...with the shadows of the night... ♪

...so baby take ♪ my hand it'll be all right...

Mr. Ryan captured our togetherness off the field as much as on. No moment was too mundane.

Sometimes we pretended we didn't know he was there, but generally we loved to greet him. Even the parents.

Amy

Beth

me

Beth

giving a piggyback ride to a different Amy

A different Beth

Sally

(Mr. Ryan's daughter)

Julie's baby sister

There is plenty of game footage, edited to show the main action.

The other teams' goalies appear a lot.

They are usually having a pretty bad day.

I'm not in much of the game footage, which tends to focus on offensive action. But occasionally Mr. Ryan filmed from a different angle, and I am a speck in the background.

Because, for all our togetherness, as a keeper I was often alone, apart from the team.

"It is the only position in which much of the game is spent as an observer, rather than a participant."
— James Irwin

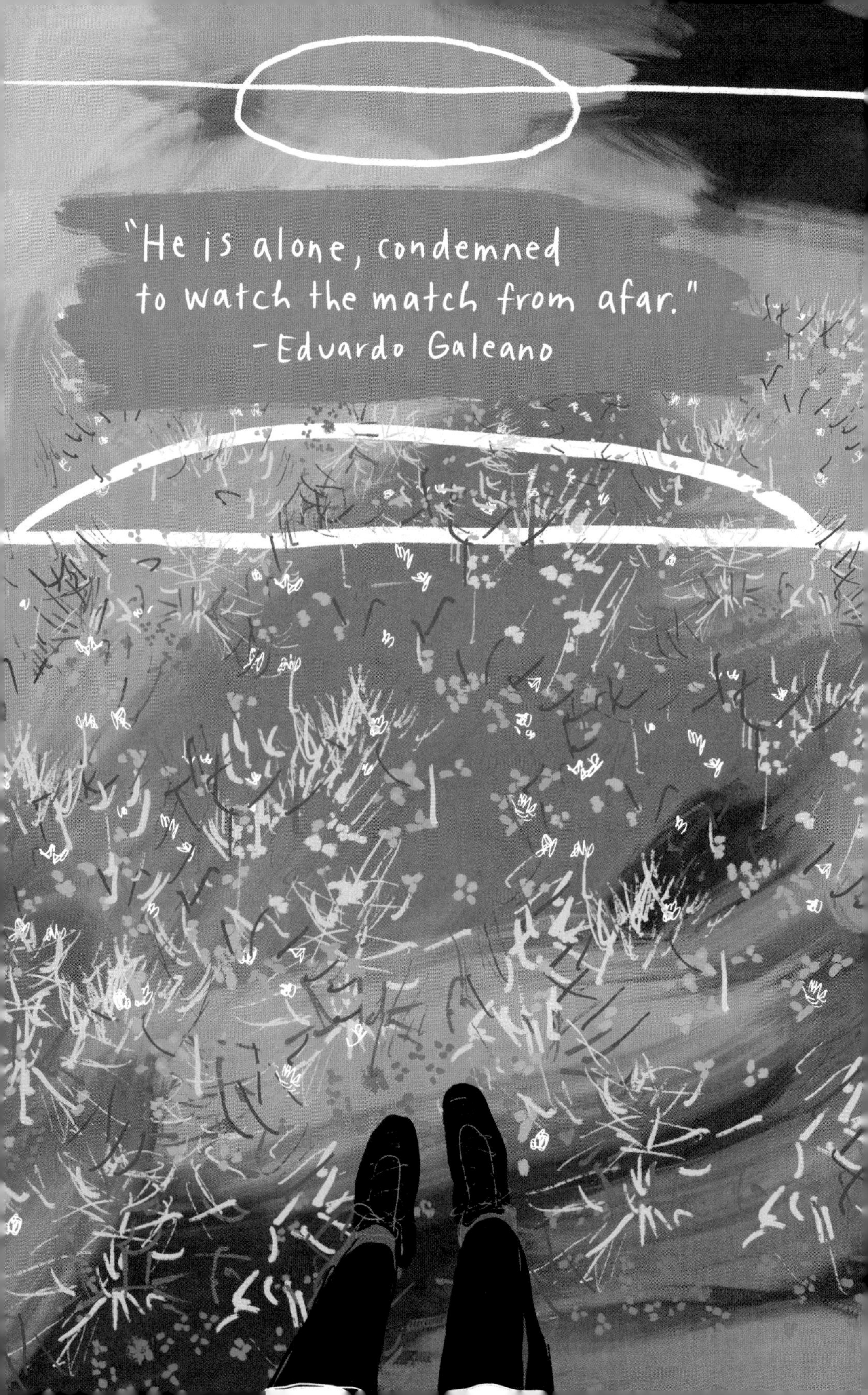
"He is alone, condemned
to watch the match from afar."
-Eduardo Galeano

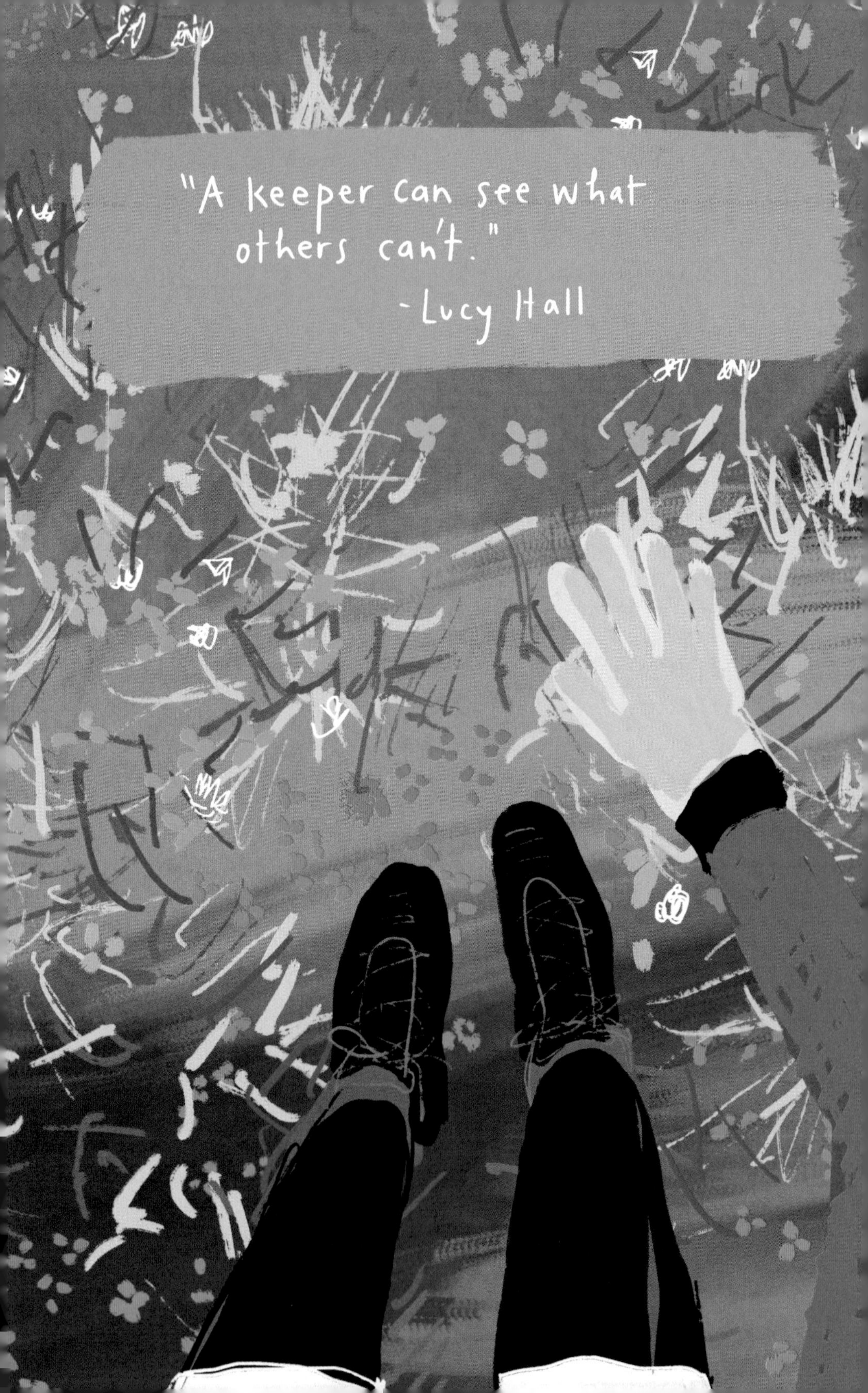
"A keeper can see what others can't."
-Lucy Hall

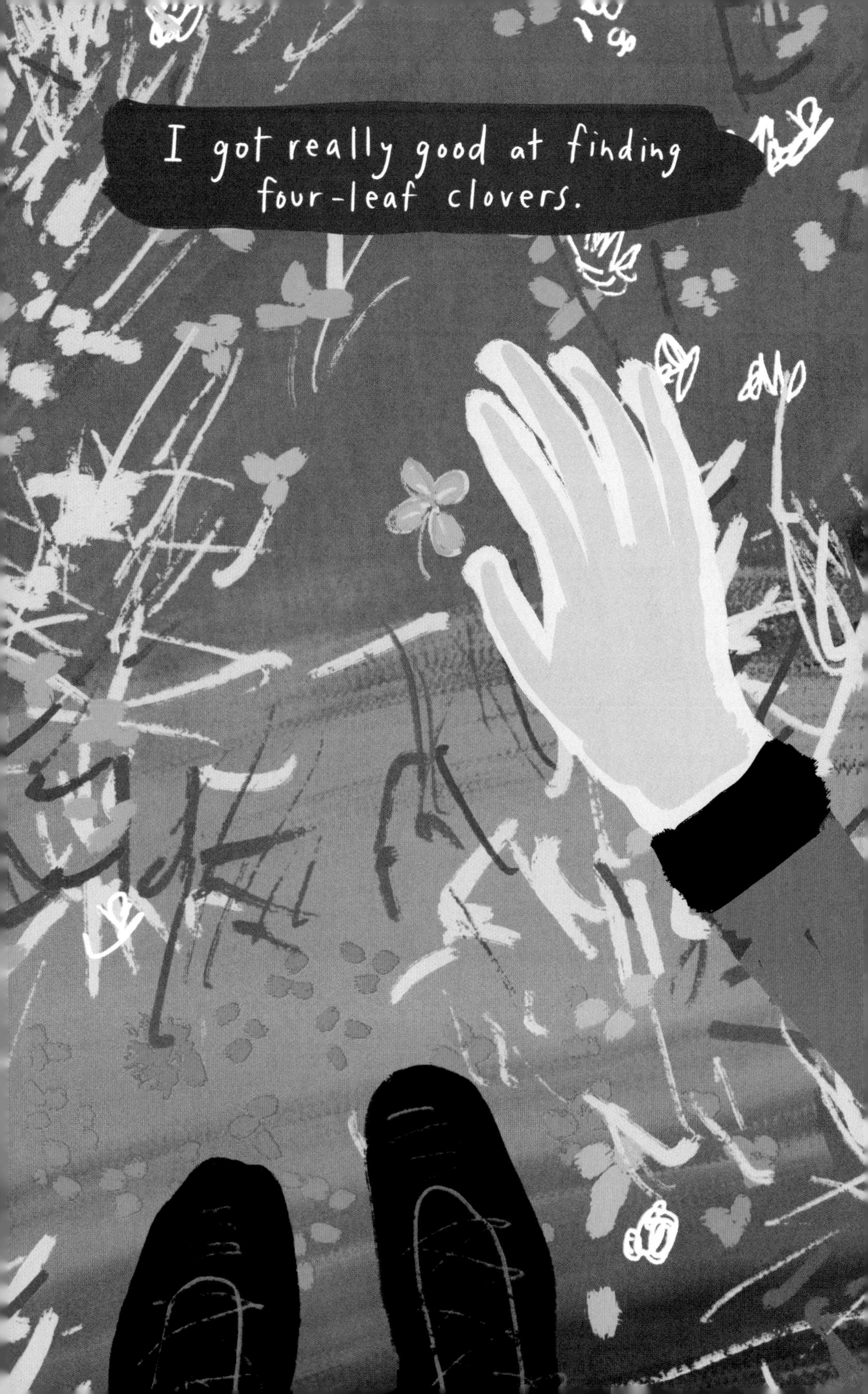
I got really good at finding four-leaf clovers.

I

collected

them

like

friends.

And one lucky day, I found

a FRIEND.

(Her actual voice! On the video!)

Jen joined the team in 8th grade, and we became instant friends.
Throughout the video, you can see us

walking together

talking together

sitting
together

me   Jen

another trophy
ceremony

Jen   me

standing
together

pregame
huddle

Or one sitting

← and
one
standing
together.

123

Inventing the selfie together.

And we were about to start
high school together.

CHAPTER

7

On Keeping a Notebook

In August 1985,

August 8 1985

1st Day of tryouts for soccer

I was 14, about to start

I really hope I
make Varsity

my freshman year of high school,

that would be awesome if I could
be on varsity

and there was one thing I wanted

more   making varsity

than

ANYTHING.

to make varsity.

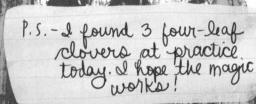

P.S. - I found 3 four-leaf
clovers at practice
today. I hope the magic
works!

The only people who attended our Cardinals games were our parents and siblings. They sat on folding chairs on one sideline, while we sat in the grass on the other.

All the games were played in bright daylight.

High school was a whole different story.

There were LIGHTS

a SCOREBOARD

BENCHES

BLEACHERS

And fans! Who were not related to us! Some of whom were BOYS!

Once we started high school, the Cardinals would split up for the fall season so we could play for our respective school teams. Five of us went to Anderson High School:

Mr. Ryan's video doesn't cover high school soccer, so I dig up my old diaries. Yikes. It's one thing to see your 14-year-old mulleted self on a video, and another to read that person's thoughts.

Five more, you can do it!

The season started with 2-a-days.

Our bodies were changing, and we were pushing them, testing their limits in the late-summer heat.

Ugh, I think I just started my period.

We noticed each other's bodies and compared ourselves to each other.

(Me? Too tall. Boobs too small.)

We noticed other bodies practicing on adjacent fields,

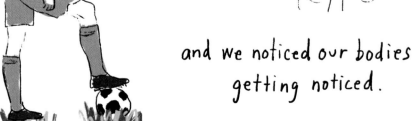

and we noticed our bodies getting noticed.

All throughout tryouts, I sized up my competition with an obsessive focus on their:

AGE (older and more experienced),

michelle looks OK & Emily looks good, & they're older and more experienced

HEIGHT (very short, semi short),

Emily very short
Carrie not good punts, semi short

and PUNTS (not good, not great, suck).

Michelle & Carrie didn't have great punts

Barb over commits herself
michelle - punts suck

But alas, tryouts ended and I:

made reserve soccer team.

In 1985, Title IX was a teenager too.

According to my research,* my high school's girls' soccer program was formed in 1979, making it one of thousands of sports programs created for girls in the first decade of Title IX.

If I'd been born just 7 years earlier, there wouldn't have been a school team—or a Cardinals team—for me to play on.

←→ ancestry.com/collections

ANDERSONIAN
1978

* looking at "Sports" sections of my school's yearbooks on ancestry.com

The new programs were a major advancement, but there was a long way to go.

At one of our games early in the season,
fans of both teams erupted in simultaneous cheers.

Pete Rose had just gotten his 4,192nd hit,
breaking a record held by Ty Cobb since 1928.

Rose was a hometown player-manager for the Reds,
and it was a proud Cincinnati moment. It was
also a reminder—as our fans turned up their
transistor radios— of what was <u>really</u> important.

Baseball.
Dudes.

There was another thing that happened in sports in 1985, though no one heard about it. The U.S. Women's National Soccer Team was born. It was put together hastily as a result of an invitation to play in a small international tournament taking place just one week later.

WOULD YOU LIKE TO COMPETE IN OUR TOURNAMENT?

WE NEVER REFUSE A CHALLENGE.

SEE YOU IN A WEEK! CIAO!

MIKE, ITALY CALLED. CAN YOU GET A TEAM TOGETHER?

DONE.

The players were given used men's uniforms.

THEY LOOKED LIKE LITTLE GORILLAS. WE WERE UP 'TIL 12 OR 1 SEWING, FITTING EVERYTHING TO SIZE.

Mike Ryan, 1st USWNT coach

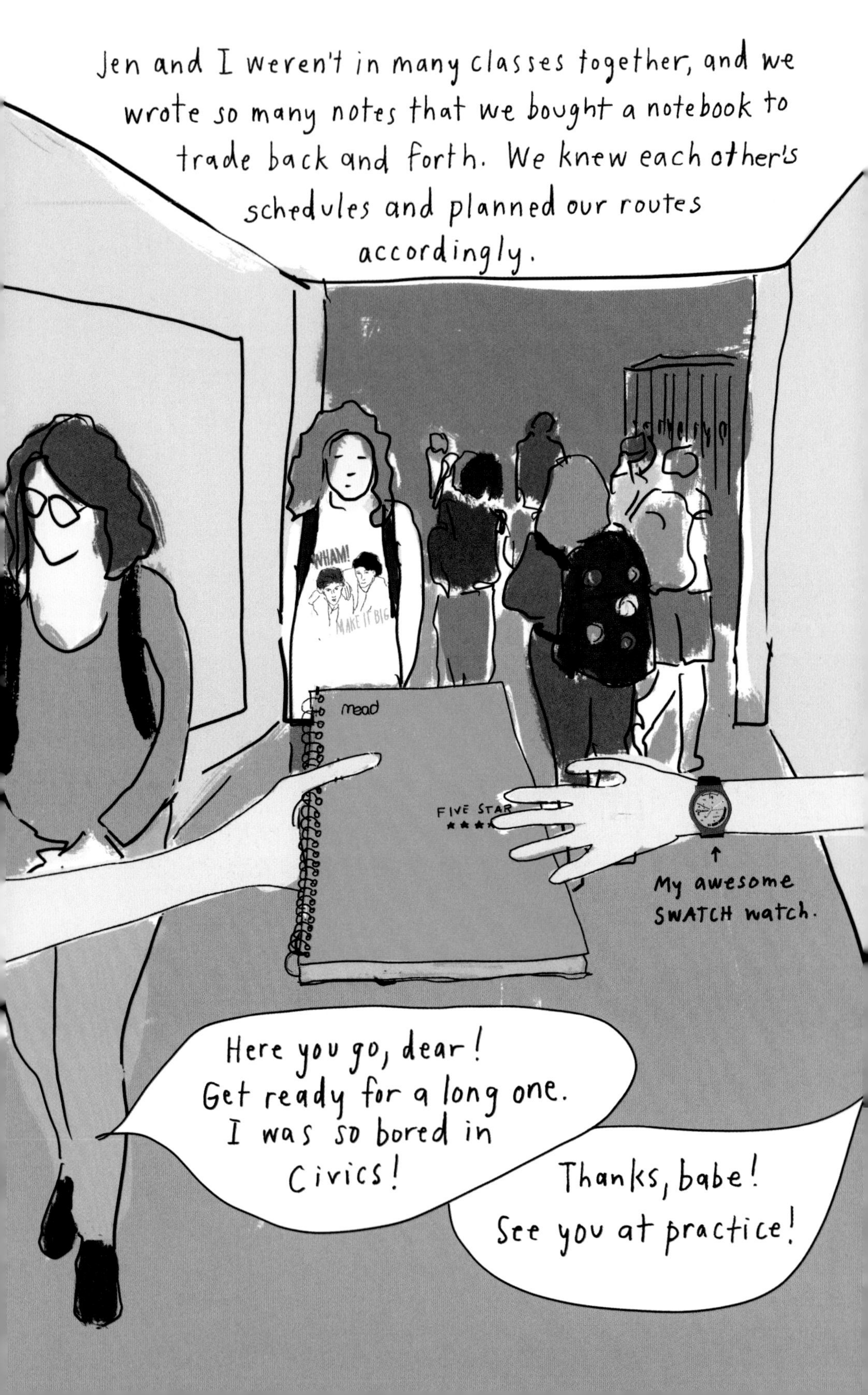
Jen and I weren't in many classes together, and we wrote so many notes that we bought a notebook to trade back and forth. We knew each other's schedules and planned our routes accordingly.
WHAM!
MAKE IT BIG
mead
FIVE STAR
↑ My awesome SWATCH watch.
Here you go, dear! Get ready for a long one. I was so bored in Civics!
Thanks, babe! See you at practice!

The new U.S. women's soccer team lost 3 of their 4 games in Italy.

Our freshman class's Thumbelina float lost to the sophomores, whose Old Woman in a Shoe called for the football team to "STOMP THE AVIATORS."

I went to Homecoming with a boy I didn't like. And I never got chosen for Homecoming court.

Sally + Alyssa did

not me   not me   tall, but not me   not me   definitely not me   also not me   still not me   uh-uh   nope

But by HOMECOMING, I —
Got moved to Varsity
and became the starting keeper.

135

It was exciting to play in front of fans, but of course they weren't all o̲u̲r fans.

As a keeper, I was often a target of their taunts.

I was self-conscious about being called Rambo and Kareem.

But it usually felt worth it the next morning in homeroom.

And at the end of the season, I had the kind of save that keepers dream about:

In the last 10 sec, the wing had a breakaway. I knew it was either make or break for me.

I stopped it!

My leg gave out. I had no control over my body.

Reporters came to me after the game & asked stuff like "what were you thinking on that last play," "how long have you played soccer" etc.

a last-second save on a breakaway in a district final.

It was also my first experience with the press.

I wanted to say "Oh shit." I wish I did. I sounded like a diz.

HEART ATTACK!

Anderson Tops No. 1 Seton, 3-2

"We have been practicing defending against breakaway shots because that's what Seton does best," Ervick said. "I was ready for the shot because Coach Hampton worked with me quite a bit. When you go one on one with another player, the most important thing is not to panic."

Anderson shocks No. 1 Saints, 3-2

Ervick, a 14-year-old, 5-10 goalie playing only her sixth varsity game, came up with a spectacular save with less than 20 seconds remaining to preserve the victory.

137

Being compared to Rambo wasn't the only way I knew I wasn't conforming to traditional gender roles. The Miss America pageant was another. In those days, it aired on network television, and I was one of the 50 million viewers.

And I had a QUESTION:

What were
my chances

of becoming
MISS AMERICA

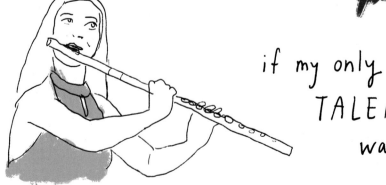

if my only
TALENT
was...

diving for soccer balls?

On the soccer field, I learned about the power of my body:

how high I could jump, how hard I could kick and punch.

But I understood that a woman's body in high heels and a swimsuit had a different kind of power.

Fast-forward to junior year, 1987.
The Cardinals had just returned from Nationals.
Five of us would be starters on varsity.

Alyssa and Sally were on Homecoming court, again.
Tracy was dating the guy Jen had a crush on,
the soccer stud with thighs like Maradona.
I was dating Scott, who hadn't broken my heart. Yet.

We were sweet sixteen, like Molly Ringwald.
We had new driver's licenses and used cars.
We were upperclassmen.
Our curfews were 30 minutes later.

141

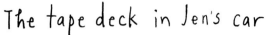
The tape deck in Jen's car

had gotten jammed
with THE BEST OF
THE DOORS cassette, and
wouldn't play anything else.

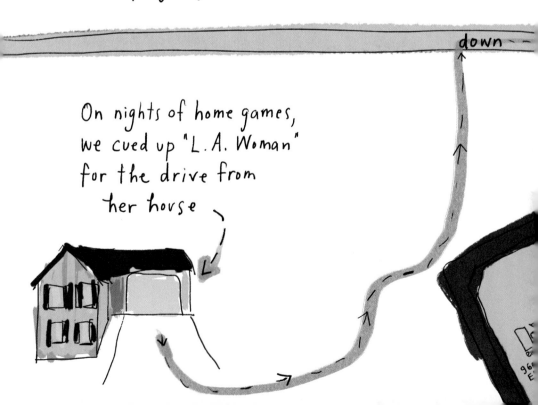

down

On nights of home games,
we cued up "L.A. Woman"
for the drive from
    her house

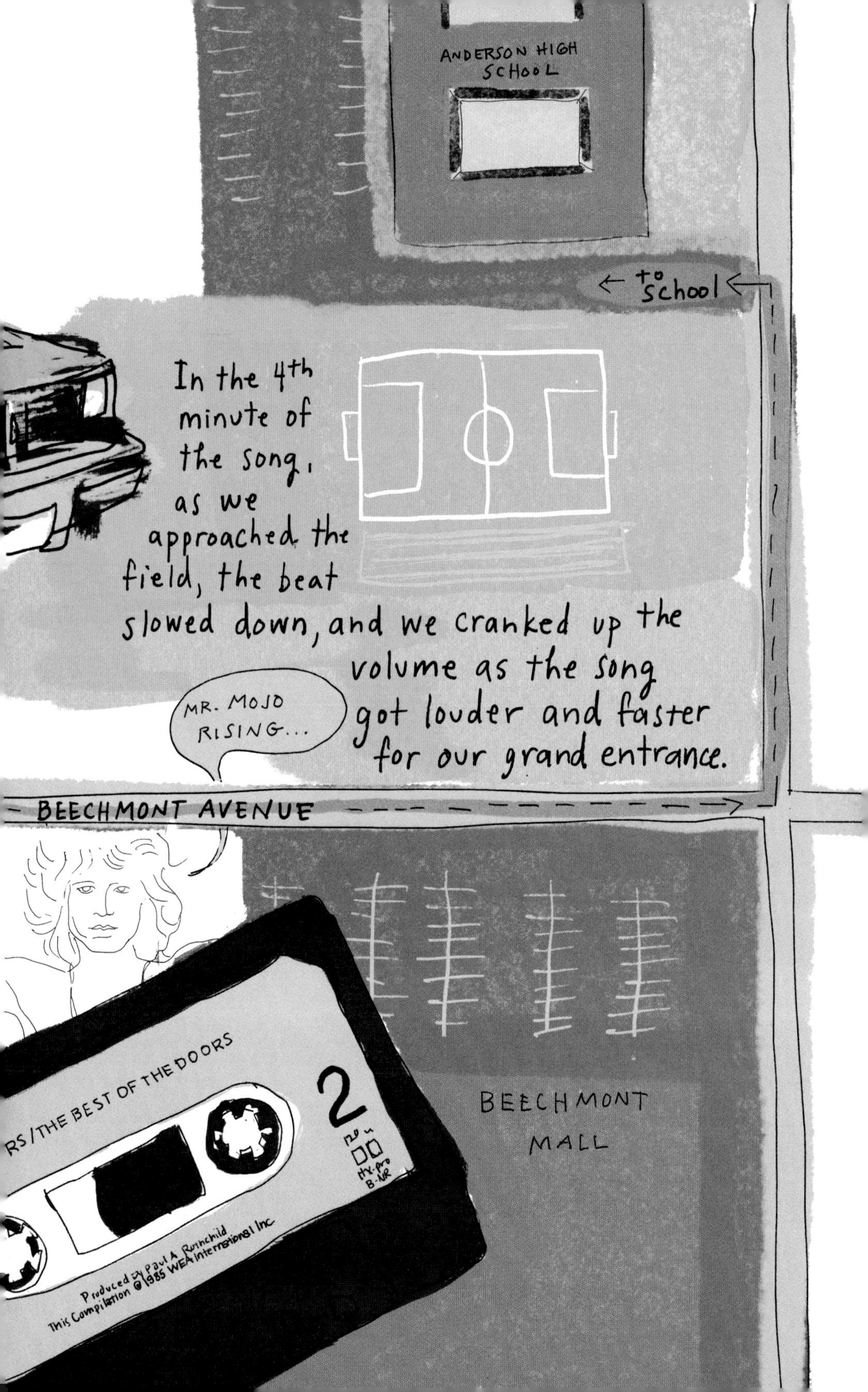
ANDERSON HIGH SCHOOL
← to School
In the 4th minute of the song, as we approached the field, the beat slowed down, and we cranked up the volume as the song got louder and faster for our grand entrance.
MR. MOJO RISING...
BEECHMONT AVENUE
RS/THE BEST OF THE DOORS
2
Produced by Paul A. Rothchild
This Compilation ©1985 WEA International Inc.
BEECHMONT MALL

The season was over in the blink of an eye, the turn of a page.

It was, according to my yearbook, "a great season." I had 10 shutouts. Jen was the leading scorer, followed by Tracy, Alyssa, and Sally.

But I didn't record any of it in my diary, where all I could talk about

was SCOTT:

I love him.

I hate him.

He called.

He didn't call.

I hope he calls.

Why didn't he call?

I didn't write about my shutouts or "L.A. Woman," or the way the sunset looked from my spot in the goal.

I read back through my journals now like I'm watching a horror movie.

Noooo!

Do you hear yourself?

That's the OPPOSITE of what you should do!

I hardly need to read my palms. I can read it all in my journals.

These journals are another form of KEEPING. In "On Keeping a Notebook," Joan Didion says:

We forget all too soon the things we thought we could never forget. We forget the loves and the betrayals alike, forget what we whispered and what we screamed, forget who we were.

But I'm not so sure I want to remember.

In my diaries, I set goals like "get tan."
And "future goals" like "get braces off."

I looked to soap operas for answers to relationship questions.
How, for example, could Reva from GUIDING LIGHT

"fall in love
all the time"?

If she was in love w/
guy like me w/
Scott how can she just
move on to Josh.

my   →
diaries

↓

I feared for my life
because Scott hadn't
called and I hated
soccer. ↘

I'm gonna die cuz
I haven't talked
to Scott. & I hate
soccer.

I hated soccer? I was burned out. I'd been a keeper for 5 years, and I was tired of being the outsider. In basketball, I was the opposite of the outsider: I was the CENTER (literally), and I loved it. Just ask my diary. ↴

I love our basketball team!

↑ THE CENTER!

Junior year we had a new coach who talked to me about playing in college. He said that 5'11" wasn't actually tall enough to be a center in college. He worked with me on my ball-handling and my outside shot, and he got scouts from nearby Dennison to faraway Yale to watch me play.

Kelcey Ervick Named Most Valuable Player

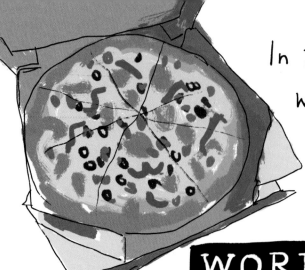

In the off-season, when we weren't playing soccer, Jen and I were playing

WORD GAMES

Impossible to interpret or understand...

Inscrutable?

(Literally quizzing each other from our vocab book for fun.)

and

BOARD GAMES

No one could beat us.

PICTIONARY PICTIONARY

Brainwash?

← our code for compound words

yes!

No way!

That's just a BLOB!

The Sadie Hawkins dance was coming up, the one where the girl asks the guy. (Is this still a thing?)

Jen and our friend Molly were over for a DIRTY DANCING sleepover. We ate popcorn and practiced the moves. (I was Patrick Swayze. I was always the guy.)

By now basketball season was over, and Scott had broken my heart. I found myself telling them about Paul, who was in my study hall, and who was, more importantly, in a band.

Jen and Molly had an idea:

Why don't you ask Paul to Sadie's?

But I hardly talk to him!

About a week after the DIRTY DANCING discussion of Sadie's, the phone rang at my mom's house.

THIS PHONE CHANGED MY LIFE TWICE

tray for pencils + chalk ↓

↑ The front was reversible!
— chalkboard
OR
— corkboard

Domino's Pizza
(513) 474-810

CINCINNATI BELL
Telephone Directory

phone book storage

Super long cord that stretched from my mom's kitchen, through the dining room, and into the bathroom for privacy.

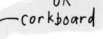

It was Paul. He said he was "calling me back," but I hadn't called him.

I realized that Jen and Molly had orchestrated the moment, and I knew what I was supposed to do. I coached myself:

If you ask him to Sadie's and he says NO, you'll forget all about this moment.

But if you ask him and he says YES, you'll end up getting married.

Uhm, would you maybe want to go to Sadie's with me?

Reader, he said YES.

In 1988, as we were about to start our senior year, a new rule was announced that would change everything: soccer players could no longer play for both a travel team and a high school team. We had to CHOOSE.

Alyssa, Tracy, and Sally

Chose Cardinals.

Jen

Chose high school.

As for me?

I continued to feel burned out.

It wasn't like I was going to play in college.

And things were getting serious with Paul.

I quit BOTH teams.

Jen ended up being the only senior on the team. But she led them all the way to the state championships at Buckeye stadium in Columbus, where she scored an amazing goal on a direct kick.

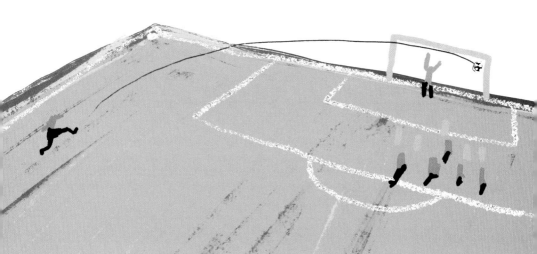

But all I could do was watch from the stands as the other team scored two goals on our freshman keeper to win the title.

I was excited for my senior basketball season to begin. I'd trained with my coach over the summer and was feeling confident in my shot and anxious to meet college scouts.

Jen was being recruited by top soccer programs, including the University of Virginia, which had reversed its former policy, that "women need not apply."

But my shots weren't hitting,

and Jen landed weirdly at an indoor soccer game.

We were staying at my mom's house that night, and as the ice melted on Jen's swollen knee, so did her dreams of playing college soccer.

And then things started going wrong with our friendship too. We went to Florida with my family for spring break. Jen had a giant cast on her knee from surgery, and she covered it with trash bags to keep it dry while she hopped on one leg in the ocean. It was hilarious, but we weren't laughing. Things were tense between us all week.

cast →

We would battle this other side of our relationship with long talks, notes, tears, and attempts to solve the problem, like a puzzle. But it wasn't a board game or a word game, or even a soccer game. It was just a part of us.

By the end of senior year,
I'd decided not to play basketball
in college. Not that I had a bunch
of great offers.

I turned down Boston College to attend nearby
Miami University, which was closer to Jen
and to Paul, both of whom would be commuting
to the University of Cincinnati in the fall.

I was as aimless as I sound.

When my senior classmates voted me
MOST ATHLETIC,

MOST
ATHLETIC

and
Kelcey Ervick

I didn't think I would ever play sports again.

"I confess I do not believe in time," said Nabokov.

But he also said:

"The prison of time is spherical

... and without exits."

After I finish watching Mr. Ryan's video, I don't believe in time either.

It has transported me back to the 1980s. In 2 hours of video, 6 years elapsed. Our lanky prepubescent fawn limbs accumulated muscles and curves. Our feathered mullets morphed into Aqua Net perms.

By the final scenes, we had lost the Nationals, lost our virginity, and lost 2 of our fathers.

And with 15 minutes left in the video,
I was lost too.

Someone else was in goal.

At first I was confused: Where was I?
Who was that?

But then I remembered: Oh, right, I'd quit.

someone
else

Jen
(rejoined Cardinals
after high school)

I watched until the end as someone
else wore my goalie jersey, someone
else stretched before a game,
someone else sat near Jen.

CHAPTER

8

Unfit for Females

1934
I detest balls.

This is Leonora Carrington at age 17, dressed for a debutante ball. She does not want to attend.

A few years later, she wrote a story about a debutante who doesn't want to go to a ball and sends a HYENA in her place.

Ring for your maid, and we'll pounce upon her and tear off her face. I'll wear her face tonight instead of mine.

After SELF-PORTRAIT (INN OF THE DAWN HORSE)

She painted this self-portrait with a hyena and ran off with MAX ERNST. She was 20 years old.

Max Ernst introduced her to the Surrealists, who viewed women as muses.

When Leonora began to feel FROZEN

and TRAPPED,

She ran away from him too.

"I didn't have time to be anyone's muse, I was too busy... learning to be an ARTIST," she said.

How did she know, at such a young age, that she could write and paint the life she wanted to live?

Cardinals—the birds—prefer to live
their entire lives within a mile
of where they were born.

They don't even leave for the winter.

Sometimes I wonder how my life
might have been different
if I'd flown away, gone to Boston College,
instead of staying closer to home.

But I didn't.
I went to Miami University in Ohio
where two things
happened.

I missed playing sports more than I ever imagined. Like, who w<u>as</u> I if I wasn't an athlete?

I PLAY SPORTS THEREFORE I AM.

Virginia Woolf
MRS. DALLOWAY

And I signed up for a course in British Modernist literature, read Virginia Woolf, T.S. Eliot, W.B. Yeats, and James Joyce, didn't understand any of it, and promptly declared myself an English major.

Things fall apart; the centre cannot hold
Hurry up please it's time
yes I said yes I will yes
(The Lady Footballer is quoting: W.B. Yeats T.S. Eliot J. Joyce)

The modernist literature I was drawn to reflected the chaos and uncertainty of the early 20th century. Men were dying on the battlefields of the Great War. Women were fighting for the right to vote, to wear pants. An influenza epidemic would soon spread across the globe. Empires would divide into nation-states. Mrs. Dalloway would buy the flowers herself.

PRESTON — Dick, Kerr Ladies established 1917

CLAYTON GREEN — Leonora Carrington born 1917

ENGLAND

Vladimir Nabokov played goalkeeper 1919-22 • CAMBRIDGE

Fragmentation and experimentation replaced the didactic and descriptive certainty of Victorian literature just as munitions replaced other products on assembly lines and women replaced men in factories.

One of the factories that transitioned to making munitions was the Dick, Kerr Co. in Preston. Hundreds of women began working there as "munitionettes."

On lunch breaks, they started playing football against the men —and winning. In 1917, they became:

THE DICK, KERR LADIES.

Their first match was played on Christmas Day 1917, in front of 10,000 spectators.

For the next several years, they traveled all over the British Isles and even to France, playing other "munitionettes" in charity matches to support the war effort.

Despite their success raising money and winning matches, they were seen by some as a "distinctly wartime novelty."

But it was no wartime novelty to these working-class women who devoted so much time to training and traveling in addition to their full-time factory work.

We would have to work in the morning, travel to play the match, then travel home again and be up early the next day.

ALICE NORRIS

It was expensive too.

It is impossible for the working girl to afford to leave work and play matches all over the country.

ALICE KELL, captain

(Source: Gail Newsham, IN A LEAGUE OF THEIR OWN!)

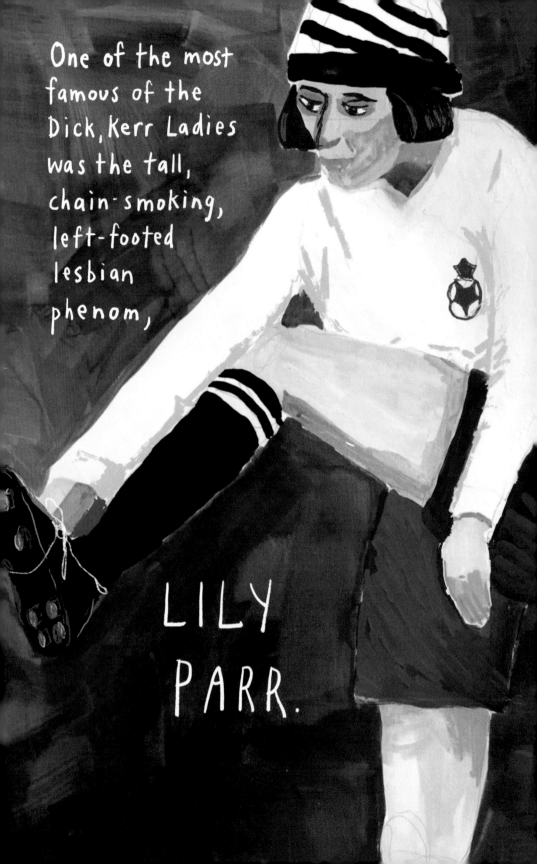

One of the most famous of the Dick, Kerr Ladies was the tall, chain-smoking, left-footed lesbian phenom,

LILY PARR.

She was just 14 when she started playing for the Dick, Kerr Ladies in 1920, and she scored 43 goals in her first season.

Meanwhile, just a few hours away, 21-year-old Vladimir Nabokov was playing football—as a goalkeeper at Trinity College—and writing poetry about it. One poem, "Football," has an English title, but was composed in Russian.

The speaker is a GOALKEEPER

The lively ball
Is kicked in a lightning curve.
The sonorous shot soars, and

whose heroic save

I leap up, blocking its
rapid flight
With a deflection.

(Translation by John Cobley)

...you couldn't know

captures the attention of a girl,
who is unaware that

That one of these
carefree players here,

DO YOU KNOW HIM?

the keeper

In silence, during the night,

is also a poet.

leisurely creates
Assonances for different ages.

Had Nabokov heard of the Dick, Kerr Ladies? It would have been hard not to.

On Boxing Day of 1920—the same year Nabokov wrote his football poem— the Dick, Kerr Ladies' match in Liverpool drew 53,000 spectators.

DICK, KERR LADIES PRACTICE

Virginia Woolf and Vanessa Bell are rumored to have attended a women's football match.

In 1921, the Dick, Kerr Ladies played 67 matches in front of 900,000 spectators.

With the war over, the men's league had started back up, but the women's teams were drawing larger crowds.

It didn't take long for the backlash—
and its predictable focus.

But what about
our BODIES?

And our
CLOTHES?

In her extensive history of the Dick, Kerr Ladies,
Gail Newsham calls what happened next "the
biggest sporting injustice of the century."

In 1921, the English Football Association
collected claims from medical professionals
who stated that football was dangerous
for women's bodies.

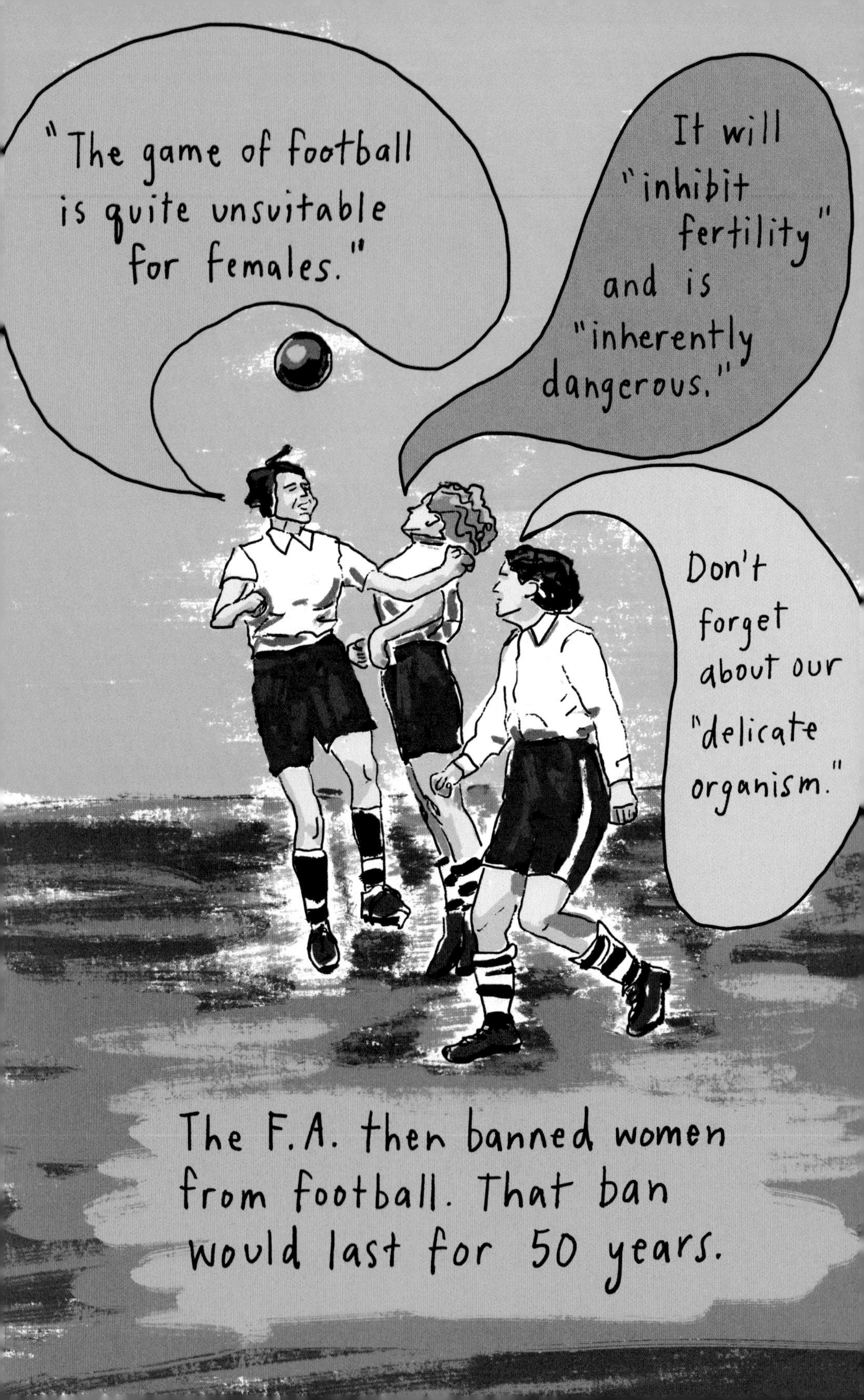
"The game of football is quite unsuitable for females."
It will "inhibit fertility" and is "inherently dangerous."
Don't forget about our "delicate organism."
The F.A. then banned women from football. That ban would last for 50 years.

The players understood what was going on.

We were all disgusted with the F.A. They said it wasn't a game for ladies but we all thought it was because we were getting the spectators the men didn't get.

ALICE WOODS
(a third Alice!)

ALICE NORRIS

We just ignored them when they said football wasn't a suitable game for ladies to play.

I think it was jealousy.

But they didn't just ignore the F.A. ban...

They fought back.

The teams held exhibition matches and invited the press and medical experts to attend.

They posed for photos mocking the ban's sexist language.

There is even a short silent film from the era that questions the F.A.'s claims.

"Quite Unfit for Females"

Football Association's view of Women Players.
What do you think?

These look fit enough.!

The players got support and surely some laughs. But they had to get strategic about finding other venues for matches. In 1922, they traveled to the U.S. to play.

ALICE WOODS

It was terribly rough crossing and all the girls were seasick. The beautiful icebergs reminded us of the TITANIC.

But the team was in for a surprise.

We didn't know till we got there that we had to play against MEN.

Soccer was gaining popularity for women on college campuses, but the U.S. didn't have women's club teams at the time.

Women Soccerites From England Play In Paterson To-day

The NEW YORK TIMES and WASHINGTON POST covered the Dick, Kerr Ladies tour, where the women went 3-3-3 versus men's teams.

The papers made special note of Lily Parr's "great speed and kicking power" and the "accuracy of her shot."

181

The Dick, Kerr Ladies (renamed the Preston Ladies) continued to play, defying the F.A. ban, for decades.

They remind me so much of my Cardinals teammates. I'd always thought WE were the first generation of competitive girls' soccer players.

Their story was almost lost forever.

DICK, KERR LADIES F. C.
THE WORLD'S CHAMPIONS. 1917-1923.

RAISED OVER £70000 FOR EX-SERVICE MEN, HOSPITALS & POOR CHILDREN. WINNERS OF 7 SILVER CUPS & 3 SETS OF GOLD MEDALS.

They were footballers, they were friends. They were teammates, roommates, and co-workers. They traveled, they laughed, they smoked and drank. They rode bikes, wore pants, worked jobs, and fell in love (sometimes with each other).

Along the way, they collected souvenirs and newspaper articles, took photographs and put them in albums, put the albums and keepsakes in suitcases, put the suitcases in the attic, closed the door to the attic, came downstairs, raised their children, spoiled their grandchildren, thought, sometimes, but rarely spoke, of their long-ago teammates, of that other life when they'd been so young and so alive, and, as the suitcases gathered dust, the former players grew older, weaker, quieter, and, finally, SILENT.

Then one day, decades later, a grown man stumbled upon his granny's dusty suitcase, and it all tumbled out: the boots, the balls, the souvenirs, and the STORIES.

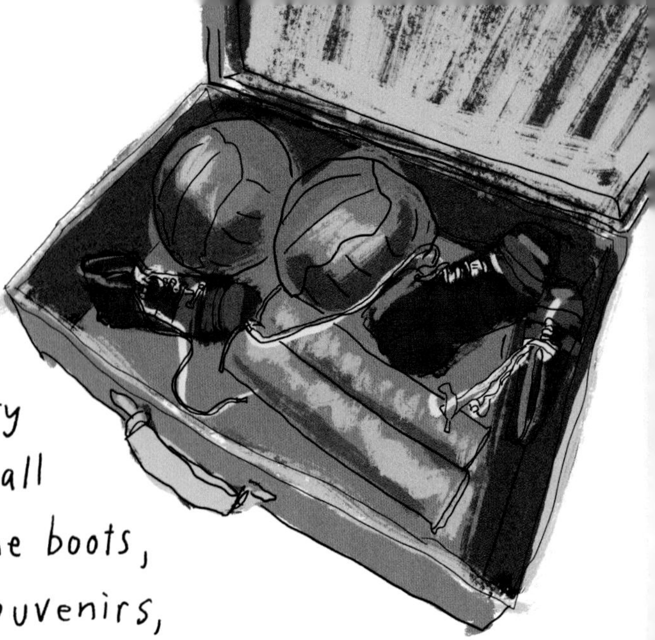

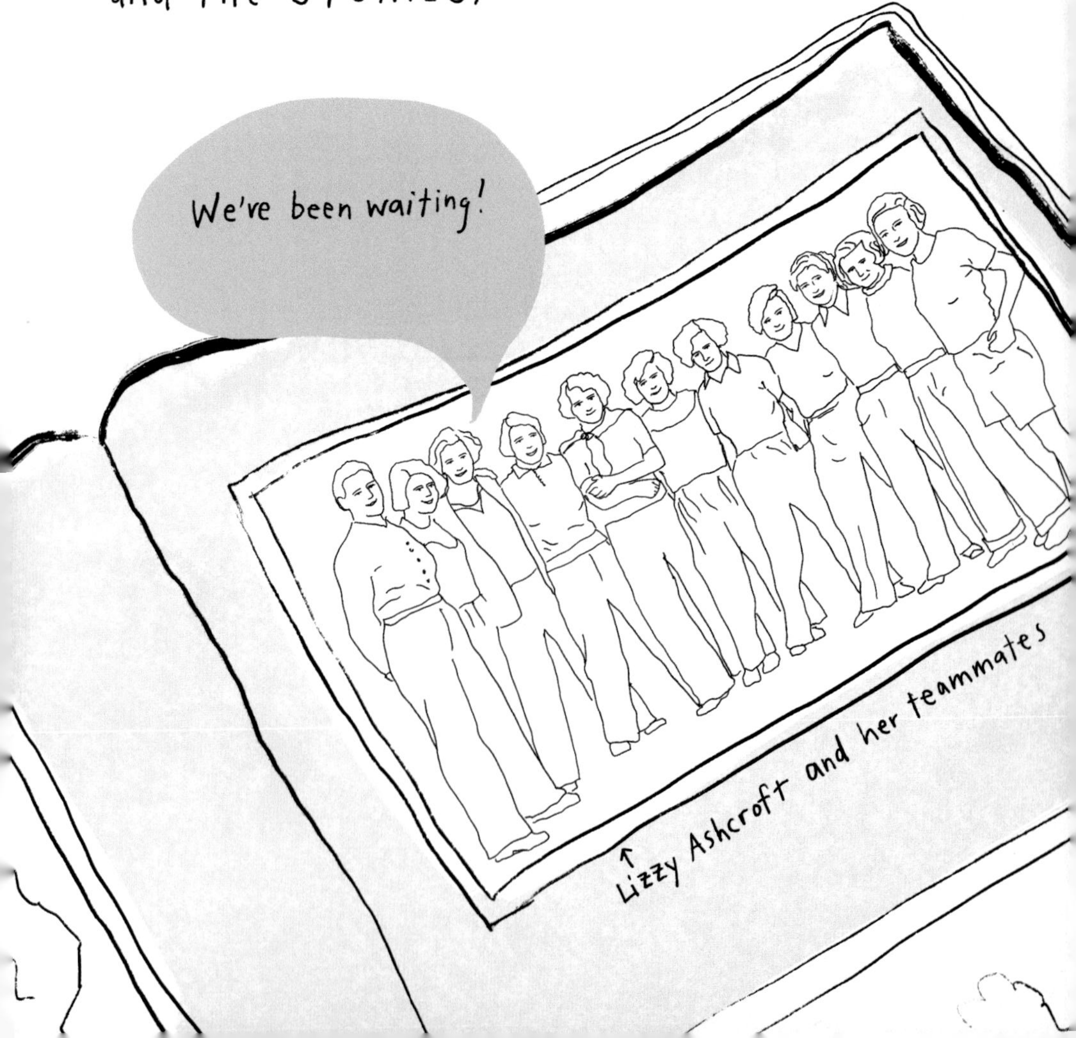
We're been waiting!
Lizzy Ashcroft and her teammates

A Portrait of the Artist as a Young Goalkeeper

One thing Camus said he learned from being a goalkeeper:

THAT A BALL NEVER ARRIVES FROM THE DIRECTION YOU EXPECTED IT.

I was at my mom's house after my first year of college when I got an UNEXPECTED call.

Kelcey? This is Tony Rocco. Do you remember me from Clermont High School?

I did. Several of my Cardinals teammates had played for him.

Can you touch your toes?

I bent down and confirmed that I could.

Good! Not all tall girls can. I'm the new women's soccer coach at Xavier University, and I want you to be my KEEPER.

And, just as I had when I was asked to be a keeper when I was 12, I said:
OKAY.
By now, Jen's knee had healed, and he'd recruited her too.

We should be ROOMIES!

Yes!

us as actual roomies in our dorm

We met our new teammates, most of whom came with nicknames. There was a magic in the newness of it all. Even though some players had been with the team for prior seasons, there was a new coach, new recruits, and a sense of possibility.

On weekends, we traveled to other universities and stayed in hotel rooms, 4 to a room.

In a weird ↗ twist, this is one of Mr. Ryan's OTHER daughters, Theresa.

Jen↑ Mary↑ me↑

For longer trips we sometimes took a charter bus, but we usually traveled in 2 university vans.

We had no cell phones to communicate, no Siri to tell us where to turn.

Bathroom break!

We got so lost in IOWA that we renamed it.

WISCONSIN

FUCKING IOWA

MICHIGAN

ILLINOIS

INDIANA

OHIO

me   Jen   Wambrach

It was like a grown-up version of the CARDINALS. No weird high school dynamics, no parents, just us,

TOGETHER.

Singing, laughing, getting lost, eating at Wendy's, and dancing to  in our hotel rooms.

#1 song that fall

Ice, ice, baby!

We'd never heard of the Dick, Kerr Ladies, but just as it had for them, soccer took us places we'd never been.

Our coach Rocco was a stocky, hot-tempered Italian and former Marine. He knew how to recruit, how to exaggerate for the media, and how to make a point.

When he didn't approve of our push-ups

My 90-year-old GRANDMOTHER can do them better!

When we were out of position on the field

What is this CLUSTER-FUCK?!

When he didn't like our effort or attitude

When we were losing to our crosstown rivals at halftime

He broke the door and we had to call someone to let us out of the locker room.

SLAM!

But when he wrote me a motivational note and said I was one of his "favourite" people, he awesomely used—and made note of—the "English spelling."

We loved our very type-B assistant coach, Hank.

And we were killing it on the soccer field.

Lady Muskies off to best start in school history

We won our first 10 games in a row, were ranked 20th in the nation, and received a letter from the NCAA saying we were in contention for a spot in the championship tournament, which Rocco called "the big show." Then we promptly lost to Vanderbilt and our conference rivals, Notre Dame.

XAVIER — S

Oh, what a Season! 13-2-2 20TH IN THE NATION

We didn't make it to the big show, but we commemorated the season on the back of a dorky sweatshirt.

It wasn't just the campus paper
that called us the

Lady Muskies.

The Lady Musketeer logo was on T-shirts,
schedules, plaques, and every page of our annual
media guide.

I don't really
wear a skirt.

LADY
MUSKETEERS

One hundred years had passed since the
"lady footballers" of the 1890s.

KNIGHTS

It was the 1990s, we'd been through
2 waves of feminism and were still
being reminded that we were
"ladies" first.

The grand tradition continues.
My daughter's high school
volleyball team?
The "Lady Knights."

Their local rivals: The "Lady Cavemen."

There's a direct line from these names to...

these inequities:

VS.

"Women's Basketball" for Women

2021
NCAA Basketball
Tournament Swag

"The Big Dance"
"March Madness"
+LOTS MORE STUFF
for Men

The problem goes deeper still.

I've so far avoided mentioning that my high school team was called the Redskins.

It took until 2020 for it to be changed, and it didn't happen without a fight.

We fight over words because words matter. I was learning that as an English major.

I was the only student-athlete who was also an English major. My bookish life always seemed at odds with my jock life.

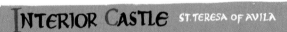
INTERIOR CASTLE ST. TERESA OF AVILA

James Joyce A Portrait of the Artist as a Young Man

THE CLOUD OF UNKNOWING

THE CANTERBURY TALES GEOFFREY CHAUCER

EDITH WHARTON ♫ THE AGE OF INNOCENCE

BELOVED TONI MORRISON

THE NORTON ANTHOLOGY
OF ENGLISH LITERATURE

Abrams · Donaldson · David · Smith
Lewalski · Adams · Logan · Monk · Lipking · Stillinger
Ford · Christ · Daiches · Stallworthy

The Riverside Shakespeare

Nabokov faced a similar tension as a goalkeeper in his university years.

The LITERARY SET... frowned upon various things I went in for, such as entomology, practical jokes, girls, and ESPECIALLY ATHLETICS.

I feel—or have willfully imagined—a connection to Nabokov.

It begins at birth.

We share a birthday, or at least a birth <u>date</u>. We were both born on April 10.

But Nabokov was born in Russia when it still observed the Julian calendar, which is 12 days behind our Gregorian calendar.

His recalculated birthday was April 22, but he added a day to coincide with that of Shakespeare, who believed poetry would outlast

SLUTTISH TIME.

In addition to our birth date is my birthplace in Ithaca, New York, where my dad had been a student-athlete at Cornell University.

In Nabokov's years of teaching at Cornell (long before I was born), he lived:

Lake Cayuga

ITHACA

← here

↖ here

↖ here

↙ here

↙ here

←— here

← here

←and here*

My first home was less than 2 miles from where Nabokov finished writing LOLITA.*

In 1991, our team took a bus to Ithaca to play in the Cornell Invitational. I was 20 years old and it was the first time I'd been to Ithaca since I was a baby.

At the Cornell Invitational, we played against UMass Amherst, whose goalie was Briana Scurry.

She would go on to be the keeper for the U.S. Women's National team, and the first Black woman and the first woman goalkeeper inducted into the National Soccer Hall of Fame.

We had another unwitting brush with future soccer fame on a different trip to upstate New York when the whole team was treated to a spaghetti dinner at the family home of our guitar-playing teammate Laura Wambach.

At one point, Wambach, as we called her, pointed to her youngest sibling, who'd just raced through the room and out to the backyard.

That's Abby. She's so good at soccer that she only plays on boys' teams.

We didn't know that Briana Scurry and Abby Wambach would go on to play for the U.S. Women's National team in multiple World Cups and Olympic games — NOT because we couldn't tell the future, but because there'd still never been an Olympics with women's soccer, or a women's World Cup.

JULIE FOUDY

Actually! The first World Cup is next month in China! I'll be playing in it!

What would eventually be considered the first Women's World Cup was played in November 1991, and Julie Foudy was there.

When she returned from China, her Stanford professor said:

You won the World Cup? Great. Here is your human biology exam.

The coach of that World Cup-winning team was Anson Dorrance, who had already won 8 out of the last 9 NCAA championships as coach at the University of North Carolina, where his team included Mia Hamm and Kristine Lilly.

Dorrance was among the first to recognize the importance of collegiate programs in building the sport because they gave women...

...a chance to play soccer, in a sense, professionally, since the coaches, uniforms, travel, etc. are paid for by the university.

← so true!

Even though we'd never heard of Title IX, it was on our side.

In the 4 years I was at Xavier, 50 (!) new NCAA Division I women's soccer programs were added.

CINCINNATI ENQUIRER Saturday, November 2, 1991

Ervick evicts goals for XU women

(Jen took shots on me for the newspaper photoshoot.)

In November 1991, the same month as the first World Cup, I was wrapping up my best-ever season and appearing in alliterative newspaper headlines.

With 9 shutouts, and a final game to play, I was poised to set a new school record and be up for All-American status.

But the ball went in over my head in the final game (that never happened!), and I didn't break the shutout record or get All-American.

LADY
MUSKETEERS

KELCEY ERVICK
XAVIER UNIVERSITY
1991 VARSITY WOMEN'S SOCCER
15-3-2 - 20TH IN THE NATION
MOST VALUABLE PLAYER

Still, we were ranked 20th in the nation again. I was MVP, All-Ohio, and most importantly, enjoying soccer more than I had in my whole life.

Dear Players,

      I think you know why I am writing this letter to you. If you don't, you are not quite aware of what faces us as a team this year. If I sound worried, I want to assure you that I am.

After 2 years of surprising everyone with our success, Rocco wanted us to play the best in the nation. Before we even left campus for the summer, he gave us a 2-page, single-spaced typed letter that is part pep talk,

Our ability level is excellent, I believe we can compete with anyone and I mean <u>anyone</u> in the nation.

part plea that we arrive in top shape physically

      be as sharp as a razor August 17th.

and mentally,

      What is that ingredient? It is the one I want you to check and see if you have, <u>this summer</u>...HEART.

and part rousing dialogue

      Why then am I worried?

      At this point you are saying, I have flipped!...Wrong!

in which he anticipates our protests

      When this happens to you, you're dead!

Now you say that we will get a break with Dartmouth, Wrong! They tied Cornell and beat #5 U Mass at U Mass

and tells us why we're

      Coach, you say, we need a break.

      you say, Coach we have a break!...Wrong!

Should I say more? Ok, I will.

WRONG.

      Wrong!

But the schedule was just as tough as Rocco promised.

Although we were co-captains, Jen and I were no longer roommates. She was growing closer to our teammates, and 6 of them rented a house together.

In my journals, often written in an unsteady hand on the road to or from games, I was jealous ("Jen and Kat are cracking up in the next row"), annoyed ("somebody put on THE LITTLE MERMAID and everyone's singing at the top of their lungs and I can't think"), and down on myself ("I feel like another keeper would have stopped those goals").

I'm trying to avoid what comes next...

Were they rumors? Open secrets?

All the comments about Rocco having affairs, sleeping with former players, with a current player at another university, with someone's sister?

I was called into the Athletic Director's office.

I don't remember what I told them. I just remember I hated it. The hard part now is admitting that my allegiance was to HIM, not to the A.D., and not even to the women on the other side of the rumors. He'd given me soccer, sports, and my sense of self back. He was my favourite (Eng. spelling) coach, and I didn't want to lose him.

Luckily, I wasn't the one making decisions.

Luckily, the administration didn't ignore the problem or cover it up — even though Rocco had turned us into a top 20 team.

Luckily, they acted swiftly.

ALMOST 30 YEARS LATER, IN 2021, HALF OF THE COACHES IN THE NATIONAL WOMEN'S SOCCER LEAGUE WOULD BE OUSTED ON SIMILAR GROUNDS.

Rocco was gone by spring.

A sudden memory. Before every game.

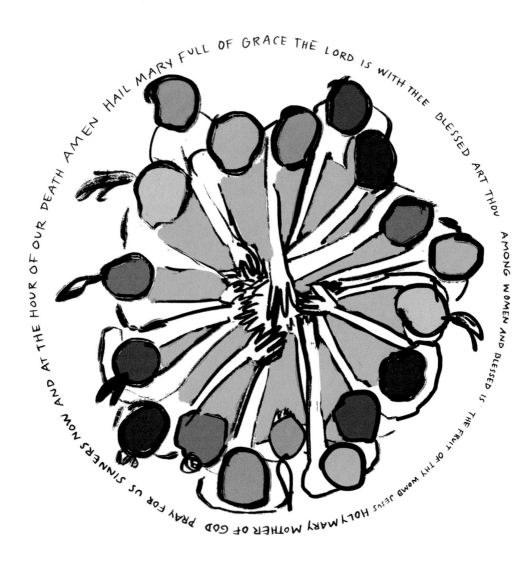

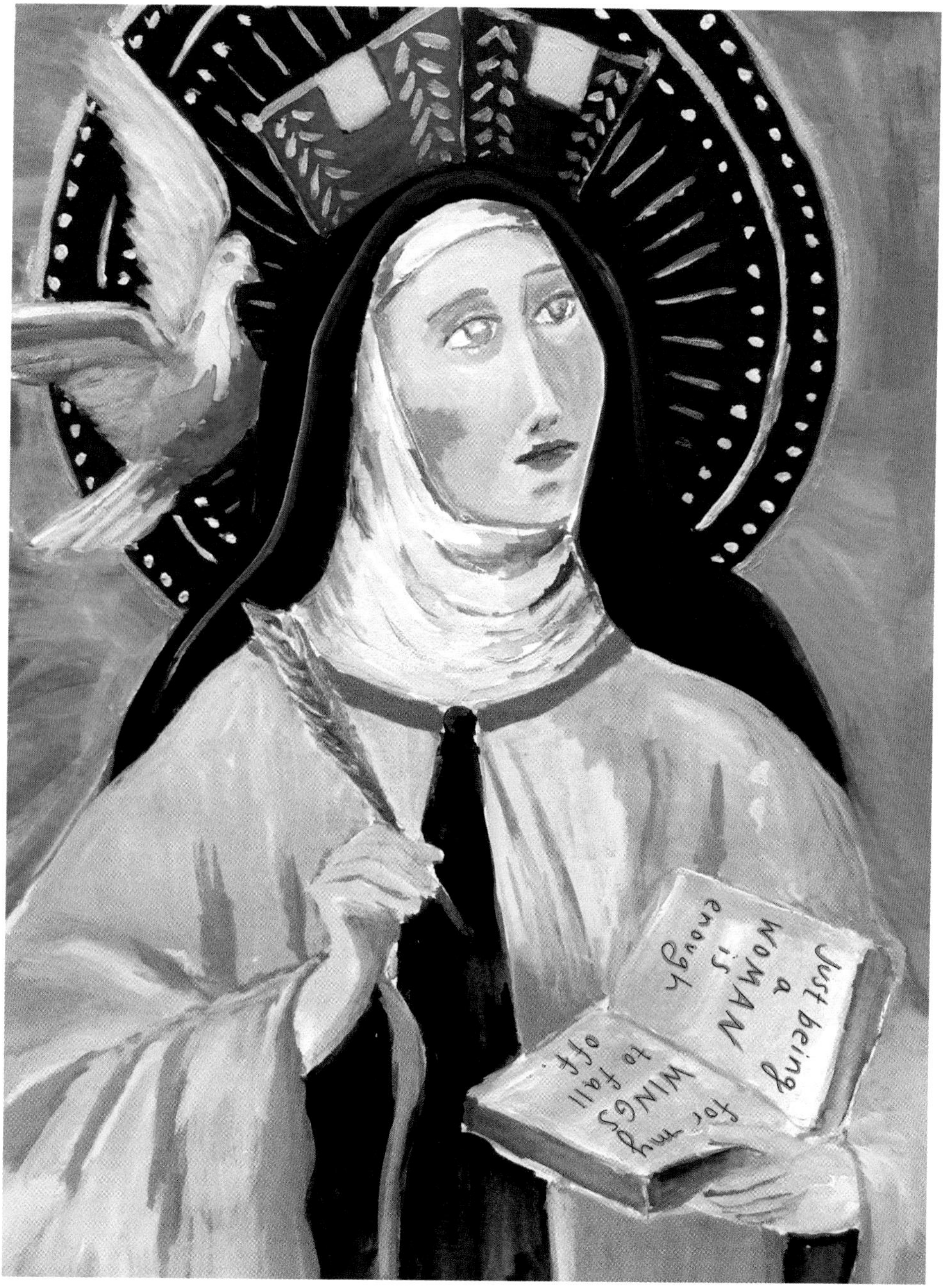
Just being
a
WOMAN
is
enough
for my
WINGS
to fall
off

St. Teresa of Avila

The coach who replaced Rocco had a very different motivational style.

DREEEAM! The impossible dreeeammm... ♪ ♪

curly wig ↙

XU

(All of our coaches were mustachioed men.)

It was a tough season for a lot of reasons, but perhaps most especially because, for the 5 of us who Rocco recruited that first year, it was to be our last.

We had spent our entire lives playing competitive soccer, and it was about to end — forever.

Jen had a secret side talent: she could SING.

I'd been dating Paul off and on since the Sadie Hawkins dance and managed to learn a few guitar chords.

Xavier Women's Soccer 1990-1993

I.
    C
We came that year, the five of us
As pieces of his plan   F
The raging bull of fire and rage   G
And alongside, the quiet man

Our trips were frequent and never dull
In "fuckin' Iowa" we got stuck
On the field these screams were no less coarse
As we formed a "clusterfuck"

And up to South Bend we went with a grin
Not quite knowing what was in store
And though we played our little hearts out
They somehow managed to get four

We tasted success - but just a bit
The Bid, we came oh so close
And we learned that you don't get a chance at the show
By playing teams like Canisius

REFRAIN

So, Jen and I took the end-of-season senior poem to the next level: we wrote a SONG. We performed it for our teammates in the hotel room after our last game.

We barely made it through the song because we were crying so hard. (Also it was a very long song!) Afterwards, with our faces puffy and our eyes still wet with tears, we struggled to smile for a photo.

We knew we wouldn't play competitive soccer any longer. Did Jen and I also know that we wouldn't be friends much longer?

That, after 10 years, 3 soccer teams,
4 spiral notebooks full of letters,
dozens of road trips and concerts,
countless pizzas and Pictionary games,
late nights talking and laughing,
we would soon call it quits?
And this time it would stick.

In what was both a satisfying and unsatisfying conclusion to my soccer career, I went to Nationals again with the Cardinals in 1994.

It was nothing like when we went in 1987. There were no banquets, no parades, not even any parents.

Cardinals go to nationals

But, according to the program in my mom's Cardinals box, there were 2 future captains of the U.S. Women's National team there: Julie Foudy and Kristine Lilly.

They would go on to make soccer history.

My life was about to go in a very different direction.

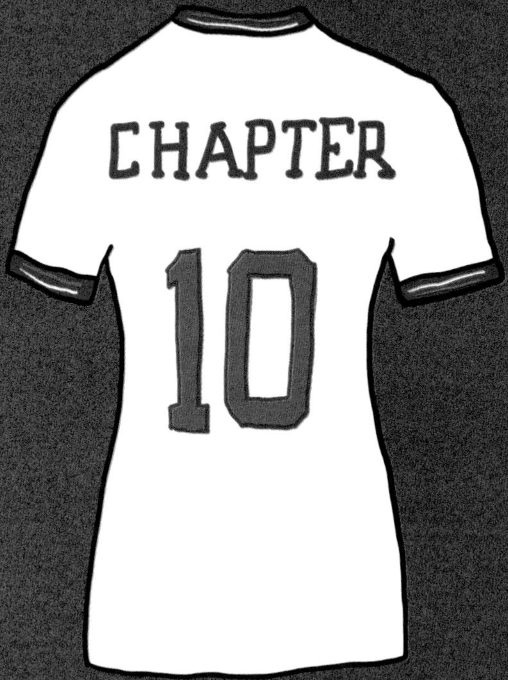
CHAPTER
10

The Awakening

In 1995, world soccer's governing body, FIFA, declared:
THE FUTURE IS FEMININE.

That was the year I married Paul and replaced my goalie gloves with a wedding ring. I was 24.

I wasted an entire day trying to find size 11 wedding shoes before deciding to go barefoot.

We got married at a park where we liked to hike.

Jen sang.

It rained all day.

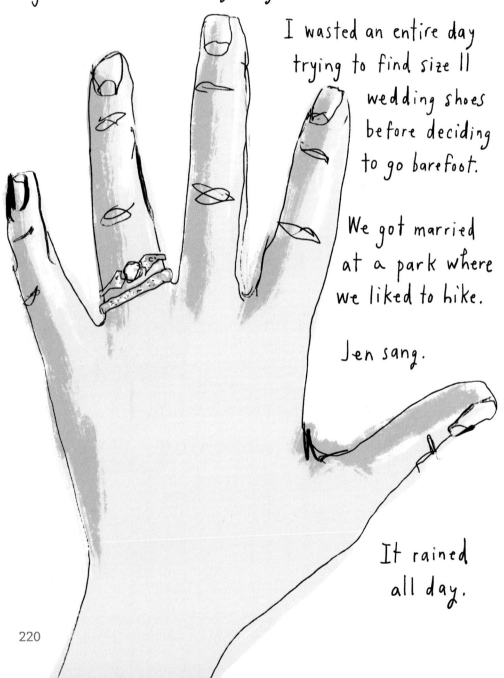

A year later, a friend would come to my apartment in tears because she desperately wanted to have a baby but her husband wasn't ready.

"I can't even imagine having a baby right now," I said, unhelpfully.

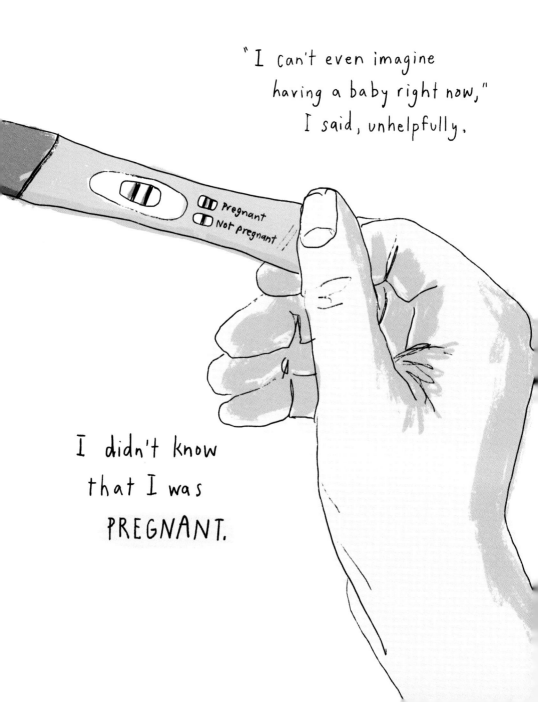

I didn't know that I was PREGNANT.

My future was about to get really fucking feminine.

(I'm still traumatized by my first visit to the "girls" aisle at Toys Я Us.)

But for now I was dealing with other changes. I had a new last name and a new job.

The former "Top Scholar-Athlete" had become a "Tired Teacher-Coach."

TIRED
TEACHER-COACH
1995-96

(Not an actual award.)

I'd gotten a job teaching high school English: 150 students, 6 classes, and 3 preps PER DAY.

After school, I coached freshman girls' basketball. I drew plays on a clipboard, blew a whistle, and repeated phrases I'd heard my own coaches say, like:

I want to see some hustle!

SONY

When all I wanted to do was go home and watch MELROSE PLACE.

223

Nearly half of my students were Black, and as I was learning what it meant to be an adult, a woman, a wife, a teacher, a coach, I was beginning to learn what it meant to be white. I read everything I could by Maya Angelou.

I'M A WOMAN PHENOMENALLY. PHENOMENAL WOMAN, THAT'S ME.

WE HAVE LIVED A PAINFUL HISTORY— EQUALITY, AND I WILL BE FREE.

I bought a cassette recording of her performing her poems, which I listened to at home and played in class.

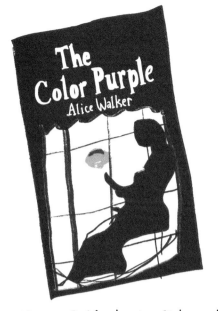

Most of the books I'd read as an English major were by dead white men. As I read and taught Black writers, I was learning about everything from double consciousness to, well, O. J. Simpson.

The O.J. Simpson trial was unfolding, and every morning as I got ready for school, I listened to the latest updates on the radio.

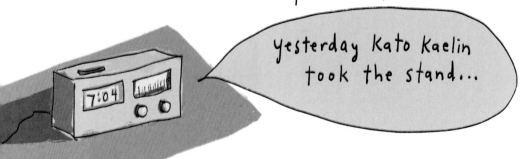

yesterday Kato Kaelin took the stand...

I knew that O.J. had been a star football player, but I primarily knew of him as the affable spokesperson for Hertz rental cars. The case struck me as a tragic example of domestic violence.

On the morning of the verdict, 2 of my white teacher-friends and I gathered all of our students into my classroom to watch the verdict live. (That seems strange to me even now, but the fact is, people gathered across the country—from outside the courthouse in L.A. to Times Square in N.Y.C.— to watch the verdict.)

Like many white people, my friends and I were in for 2 surprises:

The verdict.

And our students' joyful response.

In her memoir, Megan Rapinoe reflects on the forces that shaped her life. Her family was working class, but her parents could support their children's interests. Only later did she realize another force:

"We were also white. This might seem like stating the obvious, but I honestly think many white people don't realize they are wandering around with a four-hundred-year baked-in advantage. I know I didn't."

I didn't either. But I was learning.

Soccer in the U.S. was white too. After emerging in working-class immigrant communities, it took root in white middle-class suburbs where families could afford equipment and travel, and where there was access to land for fields.

"Soccer is not an option for a lot of African American kids," Briana Scurry said in 2017, highlighting inequities that have persisted for decades. "One of the reasons it was an option for me was because our family lived in the suburbs."

With my soccer days behind me, I was beginning to long for something more than, as Virginia Woolf described it, "the suffocating anesthetic of the suburbs."

At the time I believed that a person could be an athlete or an artist, but not both. And that it was decided for you somehow. Like the way (or so I'd been told) Soviet officials decided who would be an Olympian and in what sport.

(What can I say? I was a Cold War kid.)

I wasn't an athlete anymore.

This time, I was ready to be something else.

I didn't know how to be an artist or writer. But I knew how to be a student. So I signed up for some community education classes.

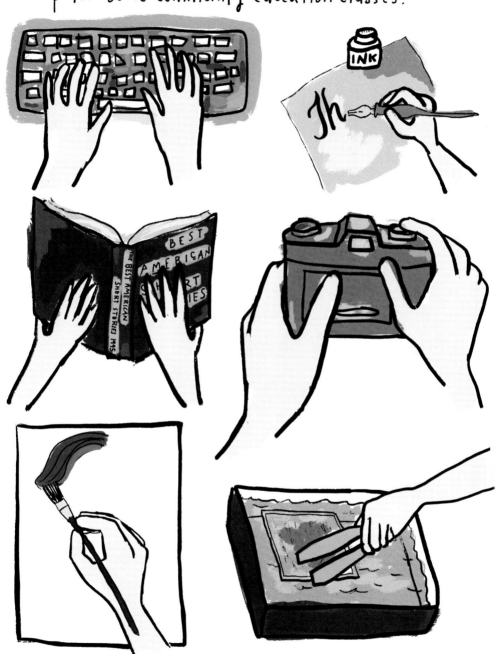

And learned new ways of using my hands.

In my own version of "bibliotherapy,"
I bought a copy of THE ARTIST'S WAY.

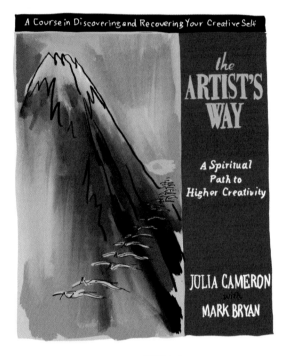

I started a new journal
dedicated to the daily
"morning pages" and
to answering weekly
prompts.

In Week 1 , when asked to identify
"enemies to creative growth," my answer?

Enemies to creative growth:
Sports!

�ᴇᴠᴇɴ an exclamation point!

Back then I believed that all the time
I'd devoted to sports had kept me from
pursuing other interests.

I worked through the first few weeks with feverish excitement.

By Week 2: I was already envisioning quitting my teaching job and going to art school.

Week 3: Paul and I visited art schools, and I was calculating finances to figure out if I could afford it.

Week 4: I quit my job. I DID IT!!

As I read that journal now, I can feel the excitement in those pages, a new future forming.

But it wouldn't be the future I expected.

Week 5: really tired   feeling barfy
uh oh: wave of nausea

Week 6:   I'm pregnant.

233

When I got pregnant in 1996, girls' and women's soccer was exploding in popularity. The NCAA added 115 new women's soccer programs in that year alone.

It was also the first year that women's soccer was an Olympic sport.* More than 76,000 spectators attended the gold-medal match at the Atlanta games.**

*Men's soccer had been part of the Olympics for 96 years—since 1900.

**But it was not aired on live TV.

Prior to the games, the U.S. women's team was offered a bonus if they won a gold medal. (They did.)

Problem was: The men's team was offered a bonus if they won any medal. (They did not.)

Outraged by the blatant inequality, team captain Julie Foudy sought advice from Billie Jean King, who'd fought similar battles in the 1970s.

You just don't play. That's the only leverage you have. ... You make them money and you have to say no.

That's what they did. Julie Foudy, Mia Hamm, Briana Scurry, and other players boycotted training camp until the Federation compromised.

They learned early that the fight for equal pay is a team sport too.

That year was also an election year with a newly named constituency:

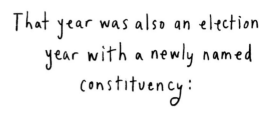

1996 "the Year of the Soccer Mom"

In 1996, I was no longer a SOCCER PLAYER.

And the winner is: soccer mom!

(Quotes from "Soccer Moms" by William Safire, Oct. 27, 1996, NY TIMES)

And not yet a MOM.

Who is this soccer mom?

Does she play soccer? No.

MOM

there are at least a million

soccer moms

I was as close
as one could get
to both—

and as far away
as one could be.

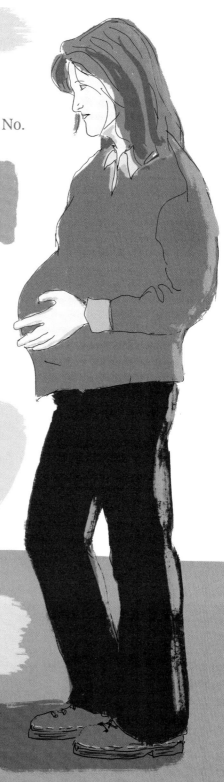

My body was changing—it was growing
another body. And the discourse about
women's bodies was as fraught as ever.

In 1996, Victoria's Secret introduced
its first Fantasy Bra—made of diamonds
and worth $1,000,000—modeled by
Claudia Schiffer's breasts.

And, in 1997, there was a new body.

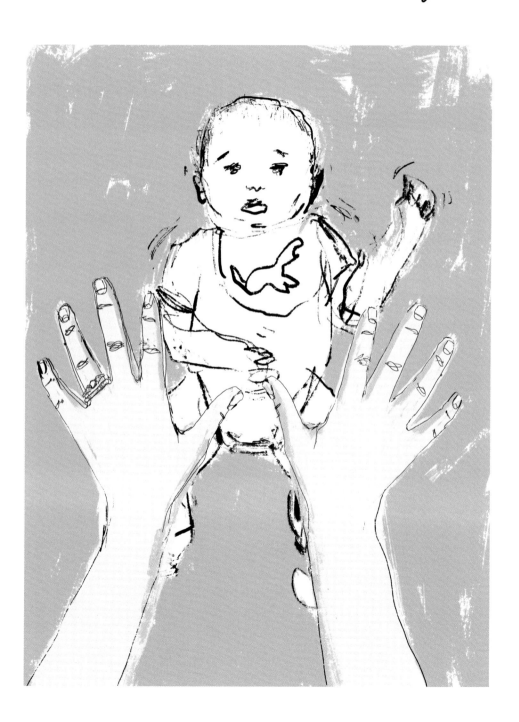

My body, her body.
She was almost nothing
but a body: crying,
eating, crawling, screaming,
pooping, sleeping, and (painful)
breastfeeding.

My body had never felt
anything like the love,
exhilaration, and exhaustion
of caring for her tiny body.

I began to notice a pattern in the questions I was asked.

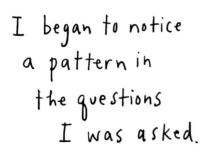

When will you give her a sibling?

Are you going to quit your job to stay home with her?

Questions that communicated expectations about my life as a woman.

Even my dumb teenage self had come
up with a better question:

But could I be happy as an
overage housewife?

So many of my female friends and co-workers
seemed desperate to find a husband
and start a family.

Was there something wrong with me
that ☑ MOTHER wasn't the
only thing I wanted to be
when I grew up?

Had my "boy's life" on the soccer field ruined me for womanhood?

The bird that would soar over the level plain of tradition and prejudice must have strong wings.

Had literature?

And then it was 1999,
just like PRINCE had promised.

1999. My daughter was 2. Walking, talking, sleeping in a big-girl bed.

1999. In my journal, I express both hope for and concerns about my marriage.

1999. The Women's World Cup was coming to the U.S. — the biggest soccer event, men's or women's, in our history.

1999. Women were being celebrated as athletes!

1999. Women athletes were getting endorsement deals!

1999. Women were —

1999. Women —

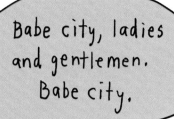

Babe city, ladies and gentlemen. Babe city.

Soccer MOMS? Soccer MAMAS!

(David Letterman talking about the U.S. Women's National Team.)

PARTY OVER, OOPS, OUT OF TIME.

In the lead-up to the World Cup,
the media devoted as much attention
to the U.S. Women's National Team's
LOOKS as to its play.

U.S. Team Looking Good: Sex Appeal Part of the Story

Success of the '99 Women's World Cup Is... Looking Good

Uncover Story: Soccer Has Sex Appeal

Talented & Sexy: U.S. Team Has It All

The Babe Factor in Soccer Team's Success

Get Real: Sex Appeal Does Count

Talented, Athletic, Sexy— That's the U.S. Soccer Team

A FINE ALL-ROUND PLAYER.

(Newspaper headlines for
the 1999 Women's World Cup
collected by Caitlin Murray
in THE NATIONAL TEAM.)

SOCCER
Barbie®

The 1999 World Cup Barbie
endorsed by Mia Hamm

One columnist even claimed that
the Women's World Cup was played
more "like the talent competition
in the MISS AMERICA pageant
than... a sporting event."

The winner of the 1999 Miss America pageant.

The winning goal-scorer of the 1999 World Cup.

When Brandi Chastain spontaneously ripped off her jersey after scoring the winning penalty kick, she had no idea that her sports bra would be more talked about than that year's $10 million Fantasy Bra.

LIFE
AMERICA'S WEEKLY PICTURE MAGAZINE

Will Ferrell
EVERYBODY'S
ALL-AMERICAN

Sports bras were a relatively new invention, having been created 20 years earlier by women whose breasts hurt when they jogged.

"Why isn't there a jock strap for women?" they asked. And then they made one.

Chastain says the image of her is "a picture of confidence."

"Everything has an evolution," she said. "It's time for a REVOLUTION."

Pro footballer
Artem Dovbyk
in 2021

In Lady Florence Dixie's utopian novel, written shortly before she became president of the British Ladies' Football Club,

the REVOLUTION ends in 1900 with the main character becoming the first woman prime minister.

GLORIANA;

OR,

THE REVOLUTION OF 1900.

But the BOOK ends far in the future, in 1999...

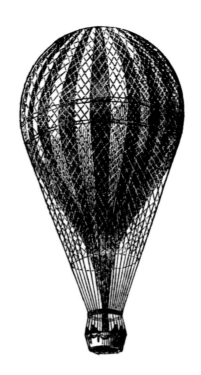

...as an air balloon flies over a London transformed by the feminist revolution.

CHAPTER X.

1999. It is a lovely scene on which that balloon looks down—

In her writing and activism, Lady Dixie advocated for women's rights and envisioned a future beyond her present reality: a future in which women could lead nations, vote, wear rational clothes, and play football.

It's almost
like
Lady Dixie

WROTE THE FUTURE

into
existence.

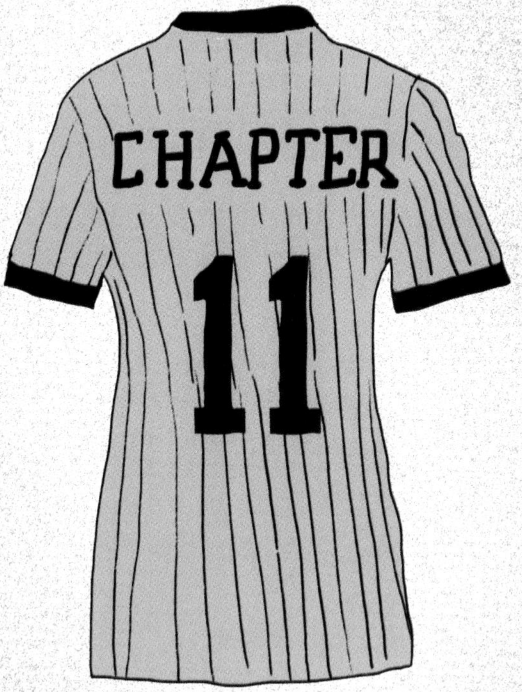
CHAPTER
11

Football Is Important

Could something be written or imagined into existence?

THE ARTIST'S WAY said it could.

Coaches had said it could: Vizualize the perfect shot, the dramatic save.

That's what Briana Scurry did in the World Cup shootout. She envisioned herself getting one save and called it before it happened.

"This is the one," she told herself as she set her stance.

I'd continued writing Morning Pages, imagining a different future for myself.

And, as a 29-year-old mother of a toddler, I quit my job—for good this time—and I went to graduate school in creative writing.

As a keeper, I was accustomed to feeling like an outsider, but in grad school, as the only mother of a young child, I often felt like I was leading 2 different lives.

In one life, I:

WORKSHOPPED STORIES,

I love the final image of her walking across the frozen lake.

WROTE LONG PAPERS WITH LONG TITLES

"That anonymous work of creation": Virginia Woolf's ORLANDO in the Age of Mechanical Reproduction

iMac

ON A TANGERINE iMAC,

AND HAD LUNCH WITH MY LITERARY IDOLS.

Lorrie Moore!

Me!

In my other life, I was:

And, I suppose it was inevitable...

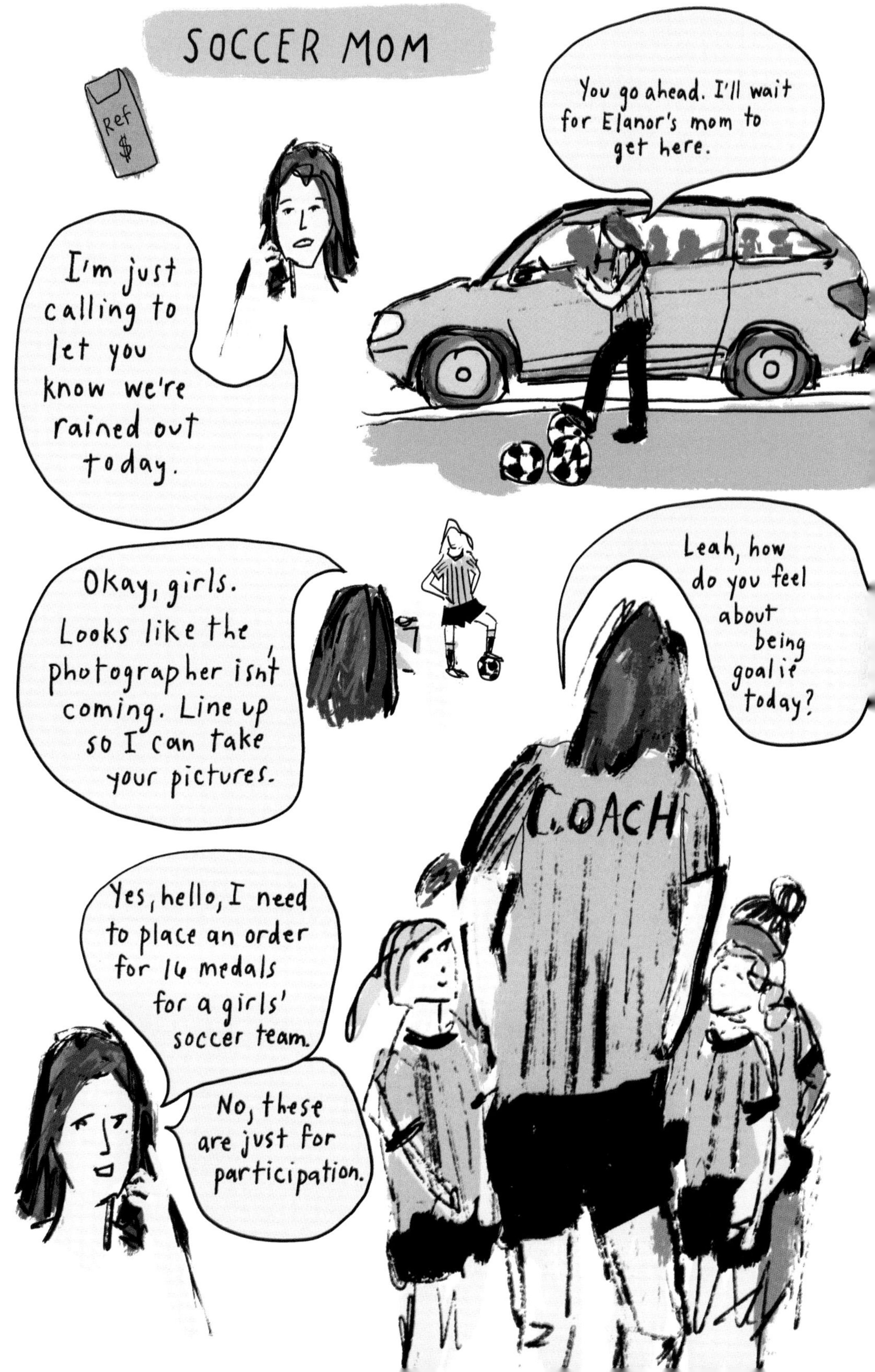
SOCCER MOM
Ref $
You go ahead. I'll wait for Elanor's mom to get here.
I'm just calling to let you know we're rained out today.
Okay, girls. Looks like the photographer isn't coming. Line up so I can take your pictures.
Leah, how do you feel about being goalie today?
COACH
Yes, hello, I need to place an order for 16 medals for a girls' soccer team.
No, these are just for participation.

In 1928, Virginia Woolf delivered the lectures that became *A ROOM OF ONE'S OWN*, which argues that patriarchal structures limit women's potential. I underlined and annotated my copy.

In both LIFE and LITERATURE, she claims:

The masculine values ...prevail.

Football and sport are 'important,'

the worship of fashion... 'trivial.'

This is an important book, the critic assumes, because it deals with war.

This is an insignificant book, because it deals with the feelings of women in a drawing room.

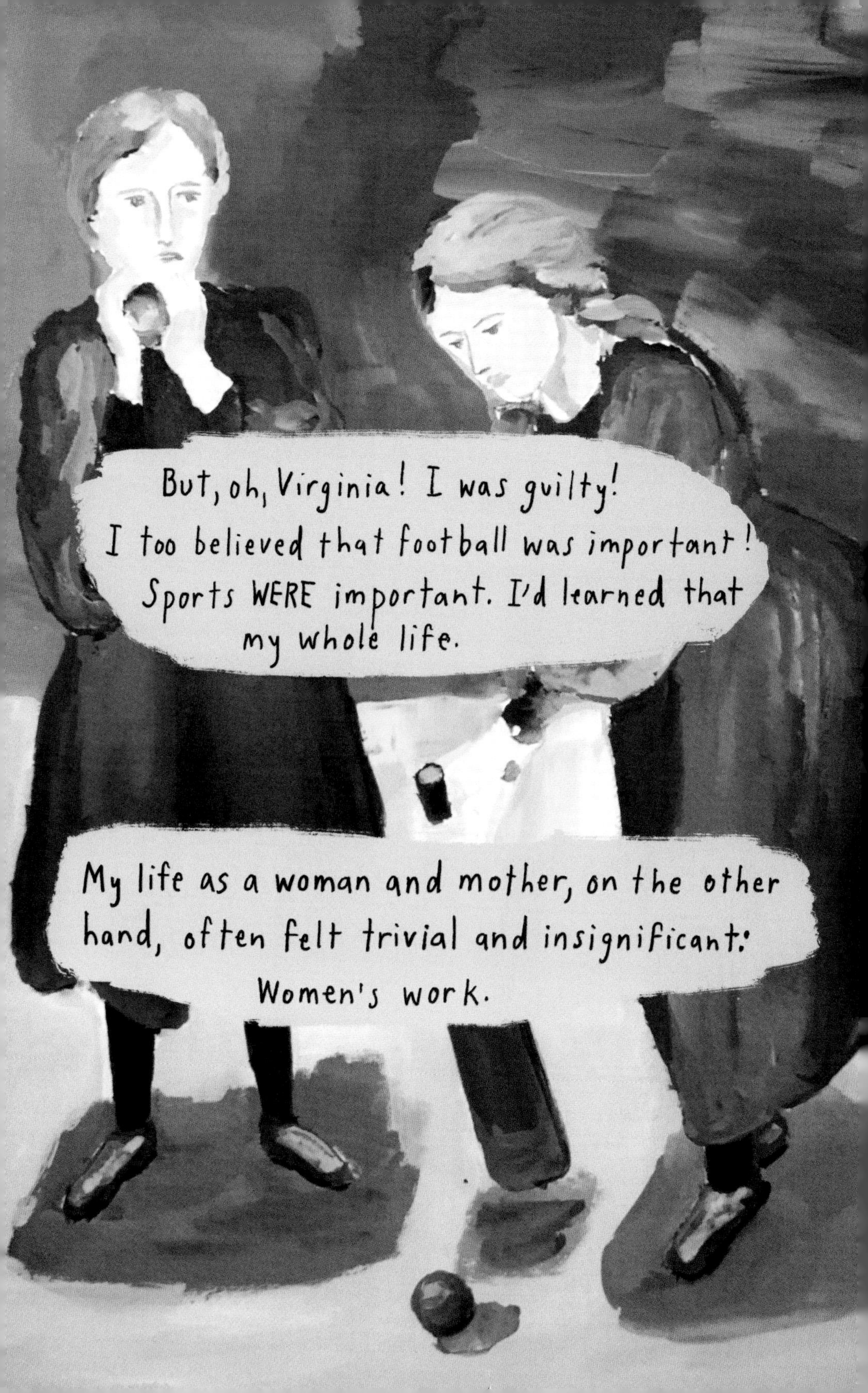
But, oh, Virginia! I was guilty! I too believed that football was important! Sports WERE important. I'd learned that my whole life.
My life as a woman and mother, on the other hand, often felt trivial and insignificant: Women's work.

All my writing professors were men, and I wanted to write like them and like the male writers that I—and they—so admired.

I was more like Nabokov than I ever knew.

I am prejudiced, in fact, against all women writers

↖ Letter from Nabokov to Edmund Wilson

And yet, it was becoming clear that the words of women writers spoke to me most directly.

Books in circle (clockwise from top): Toni Morrison, Leslie Marmon Silko, Ann Petry, Emily Brontë, Harriet Jacobs, Gertrude Stein, Frances Ellen Watkins Harper, Charlotte Perkins Gilman, Maxine Hong Kingston, Elizabeth Stuart Phelps, Ana Castillo, Zora Neale Hurston, Clarice Lispector, Zitkala-Ša, Nella Larsen, Virginia Woolf

They spoke of unlimited desire and ambition in limited and separate spheres.

They spoke of motherhood as something to be valued.

Of the kitchen as a space of creativity and community, of their words as a source of power.

They spoke of sisterhood and the bonds of women.

They spoke of injustice, of resistance, of revolution.

And in those grad school years
I found a new set of teammates—

women who supported, affirmed,
and encouraged me

in a way I'd never
experienced before.

These were hard years for my marriage.
I was focused on my daughter and school.
We were stressed about money.

When I finished my master's degree, we fought
about whether I could go for a Ph.D.— 4 more
years on a $10,000 annual stipend? It only
became possible when I got a fellowship
for twice that amount.

In 2004, Sepp Blatter, the president of FIFA, the international soccer organization, told an interviewer:

Come on, let's get women to play in more feminine garb... in tighter shorts, for example, [like] in volleyball.

Beautiful women play football nowadays, excuse me for saying so.

Our team in 2004

I don't know why I thought it was so different, being an ATHLETE and being an ARTIST.

An athlete who is a woman has more in common with an artist who is a woman than an athlete who is a man.

There is no reason why football should not be played by women.

The masculine values... prevail.

Women are not the "ornamental and useless" creatures men have pictured.

I didn't have time to be anyone's muse.

We want equal pay.

I was getting angry.

I was finding my voice.

CHAPTER

12

Conclusive Evidence

When my daughter was in 5th grade,
I again volunteered to coach her school
team. This time, another mom volunteered
too. We met in person at the first practice.

I could tell something
about her right away.

Until then I'd coached with dads (always dads) who knew little about the sport.

But Mary-Kate and I knew the same drills and could demonstrate the ball-control skills we wanted the girls to work on.

We were a new kind of SOCCER MOM.

By then I'd finished my Ph.D. and gotten a job as a creative writing professor in South Bend, Indiana.

Paul hadn't wanted to move, and neither had I, but it was a good job with a salary and benefits, which we hadn't had in years.

At the modern university with no bricks or ivy,

INDIANA UNIVERSITY SOUTH BEND

it was almost impossible to imagine how different things had been just 35 years earlier, before TITLE IX. When Bernice Sandler wasn't considered for academic jobs, when Patsy Mink was turned down by medical schools, and Marvella Hern Bayh by the University of Virginia—on the basis of sex.

I owed not just my sports career but my academic career to TITLE IX.

Aside from coaching, I hadn't thought much about women's soccer in years. I had a new identity. I was a WRITER now.

Maybe it was because I'd moved to the town of our former Xavier rivals, Notre Dame, or because their women's soccer team was the best in the country (though you'd never know it because all anyone could talk about was the football team), or because time passes and you start looking back, or maybe I just needed a distraction from my marriage.

Anyway. I started tuning into women's soccer.

It didn't take long to spot
a name I recognized.

I was a bit slow to figure it out, but once I saw her talk in interviews, I knew Abby Wambach was the younger sister of my gregarious, goal-scoring, guitar-playing teammate.

OMG, that must be the younger sister we met at Wambach's house!

I loved watching HOPE SOLO.

Was there ever a more perfect name
for a goalkeeper?

Three O's like soccer balls,
the ever-important HOPE, and the
existential state of the keeper: SOLO.

Years later when I read her memoir, I felt an added sense of kinship. She said that her discomfort in group situations made her feel dysfunctional. Then she read an article that she said felt like a "master's thesis" on her personality.

Did I enjoy spending time alone or with just one or two friends?

CHECK.

Was I exhausted and drained by too much social contact?

CHECK.

She learned that she wasn't dysfunctional; she was an INTROVERT.

Was I uncomfortable around other mothers because I was an INTROVERT?

We heard you wrote a book. What's it about?

Or because I was AMBITIOUS?

Uhm, it's a story collection about motherhood. Like, in one story a mother gives up her husband and kids for Lent.

Catholic moms ←

Or was I just AWKWARD?

In those years, my life outside of work

revolved around my daughter's.

And I was the primary breadwinner.

So, why did having a meaningful career that I loved

make me feel like a BAD MOM?

As I was uncovering a new self, I felt an increasing distance between me and my old self, the one before I'd become a mother, a wife, a writer, a professor.

Over the years, I sometimes took my daughter's team to watch the Notre Dame women's soccer team play. I would drift away from the team to the bleachers behind the goal—my favorite familiar vantage point. In front of me was the very field I'd played on nearly 20 years earlier, the goal I'd defended.

I could almost see my former self out on that field. Almost feel the ball in my soft goalie gloves,

the extension of my leg as I punted the ball down-field.

I could almost hear the sound of my own voice, calling to my teammates:

MAN ON,
DROP BACK,
CHANGE
FIELDS.

Mom!
But I was called back to the present, my new self.
There you are! I've been looking for you.
You know I've played on this field, right?
She did know.
I liked to remind her of evidence that I existed before her.
Yeah, I know, Mom. Can I have some money for hot chocolate?

The original title of Nabokov's memoir,

SPEAK, MEMORY,

was: CONCLUSIVE EVIDENCE.

"Of my having existed," he explained.

I sometimes Googled my old self, my maiden name, searching, I suppose, for evidence of her existence. But that self existed in a pre-Internet era, and the only things that came up were Xavier soccer stats, including whichever of my school records hadn't been broken yet by another keeper.

Maybe I sensed that my new self was missing some part of that old athlete self, the one I'd left behind in pursuit of becoming a writer.

I hadn't even really EXERCISED since my daughter was born.

I'd been writing books about women whose existence had been forgotten.

I was unhappy in my marriage.

I'd been Kelcey Parker for 2 books and nearly 2 decades.

Maybe it was time to be KELCEY ERVICK again.

I had no idea how to be a new version
of an old self.

I drew on
the strengths and
skills of both
of those selves:

I visualized a new life
for myself.

I wrote.

I drew.

I joined a gym.

In 2014, I got a message on Facebook, an invitation to a CARDINALS reunion hosted by Sally — Mr. Ryan's daughter.

The next thing I knew, I was back in Cincinnati, and we were all together for the first time since we were teenagers.

Jen ↑

Me ↑

It had been 30 years, but when it was time for photos, we fell into our familiar formation.

Even though I arrived at the reunion with my own mom, I was taken aback by the sight of all the parents, and by the emotions that overcame me.

Mr. & Mrs. Carter!

Mr. & Mrs. Grunwald!

Mr. & Mrs. Ryan!

Mrs. Lynn!

Mrs. Johnson!

For the ones who were there, and the ones who are gone.

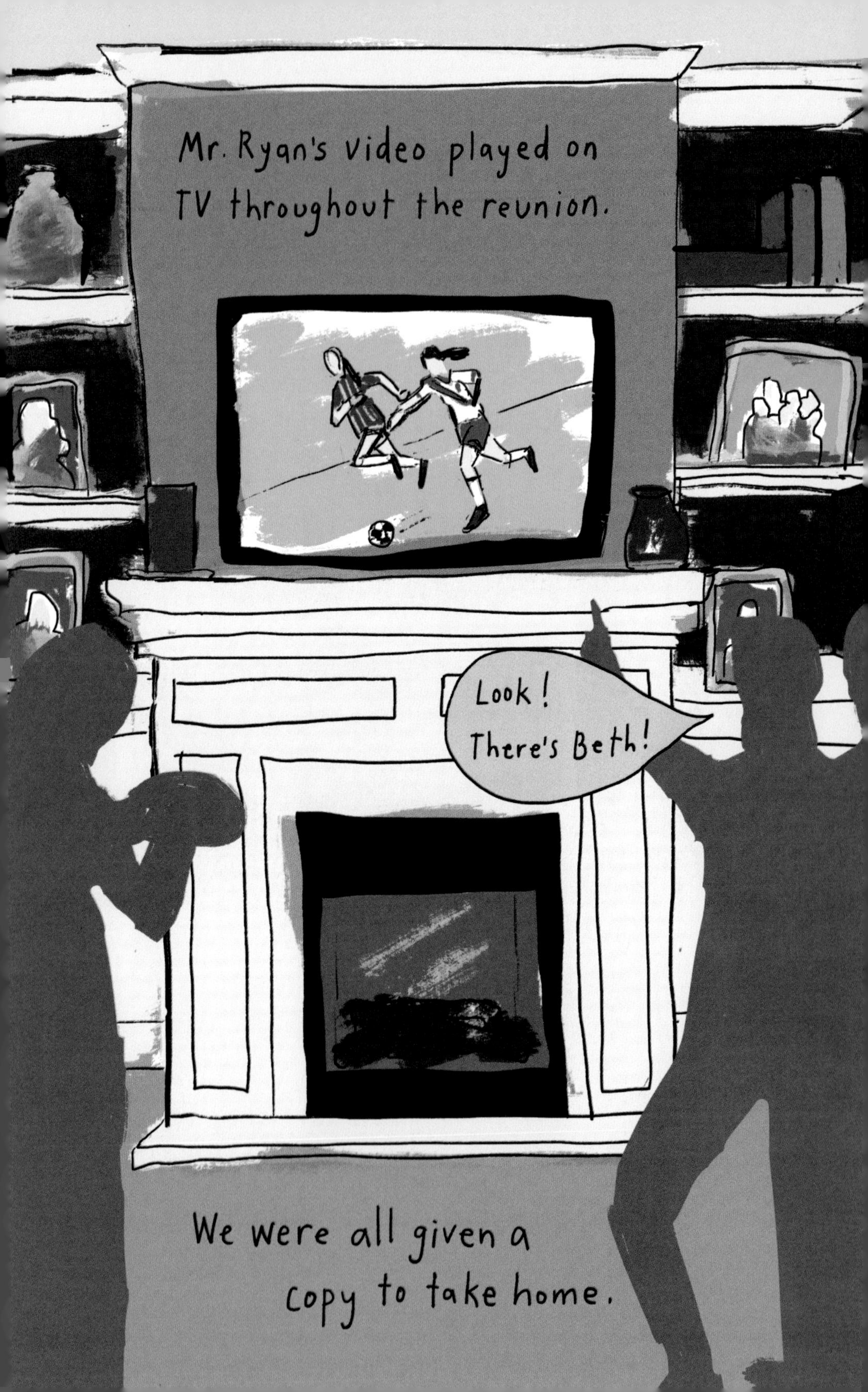
Mr. Ryan's video played on TV throughout the reunion.
Look! There's Beth!
We were all given a copy to take home.

Eventually and inevitably,
Jen and I fell into our familiar formation—
apart from the team.

I told her about my daughter,
my recent divorce.

Yeah, I was sorry to hear about that.

She told me about her husband,
her 3 boys. How she teaches
middle school and plays
sand volleyball.

Sounds like you're keeping busy!

Tell them I said hello!

She still gets together
regularly with our Xavier
teammates for
"Game Night." (board games)

I'd like to say that hindsight would give me perspective on whatever happened with Jen. But our relationship has always felt inscrutable, to invoke one of our old vocab words, and hindsight hasn't helped.

I look back to my high school diaries

We've been having bad probs + it sucks.

for clues,

It's like we can't even talk it over to work it out.

but I was just as baffled then.

We just talk in circles because both of us have valid points + reasons for acting the way we do so there's no blame to be placed, it just doesn't work.

CHAPTER

13

The Keeper's Secret

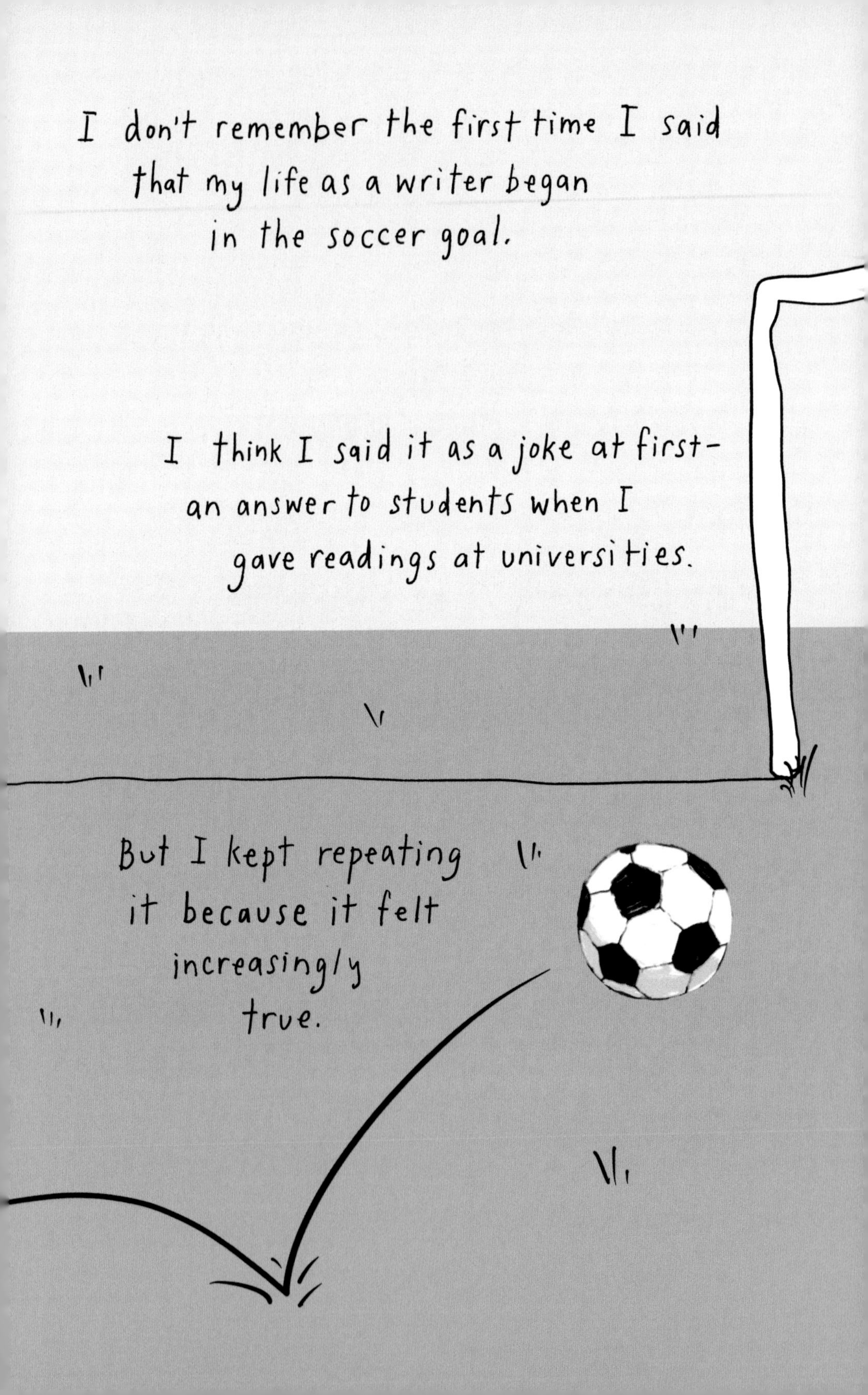
I don't remember the first time I said that my life as a writer began in the soccer goal.
I think I said it as a joke at first- an answer to students when I gave readings at universities.
But I kept repeating it because it felt increasingly true.

James Irwin says that, like goalkeeping:
"Writing is an intense psychological and philosophical pursuit,

requiring heightened senses,
understanding,
and
imagination."

In an article about Camus, Lucy Hall says:
"It is one of the most poetic crossovers imaginable:
football and literature;
the beautiful game and the written word."

For so long, I'd distanced myself from my sports past, thinking there was no place for it in my creative life. But they'd always been connected.

And consider Nabokov, who says of his goalkeeping experience:

> "I was less the keeper of a soccer goal than the keeper of a secret."

What was his secret? It was, as often happens with Nabokov, tucked in at the end of a long sentence:

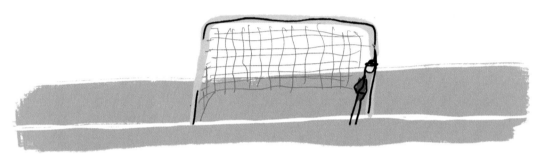

"As with folded arms I leant my back against the left goalpost, I enjoyed the luxury of closing my eyes, and thus I would ... feel the blind drizzle on my face and hear, in the distance, the broken sounds of the game and think of myself as an EXOTIC BEING in an English footballer's disguise...

... composing verse in a tongue nobody understood...

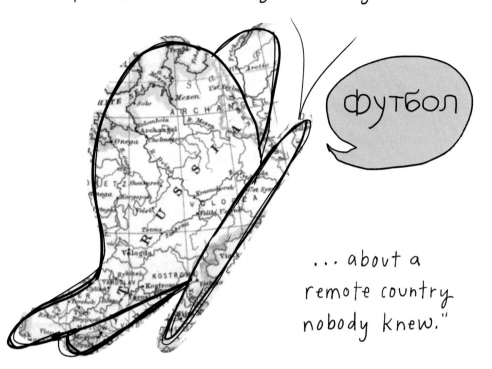

футбол

... about a
remote country
nobody knew."

Nabokov's SECRET
was that he was a WRITER.

Small wonder I was not
very popular with
my teammates.

When I took a Czech
language class in 2012,
I was happy to learn
that the Czech word
for GOALKEEPER
comes from the same
root as the Gothic
towers that protected
Prague for centuries,
like the Prašná Brána,
the Powder Tower →
where gunpowder was
stored in the 1600s.

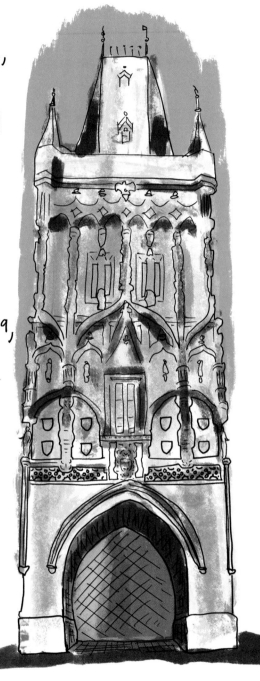

Bránit – to defend

Brána – big door/gate
BRANKAŘKA –
goalie

(My notes from
Czech class.)

This isn't too far from the English etymology, from the Middle English KEPEN— to keep, guard, look after, watch.

And isn't that the work of writers?

"The act of vividly recalling a patch of the past is something that I seem to have been performing with the utmost zest all my life."
—Nabokov

To be KEEPERS of histories, stories, memories?

"So all a man could win in the conflict between plague and life was knowledge and memories."
—Camus

But it's also important to remember that there are many pasts, many histories and memories that have yet to be told.

That it matters who tells the story,

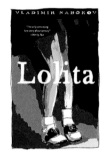

who is considered the "stranger,"

Who gets to play,

Dudes.

and who gets banned,

whose stories get forgotten,

and who gets denied admission.

These days when I think of Nabokov,
I often think of his wife, Véra.

Once an aspiring writer herself, she dedicated
her life to his writing, typing all his
novels from his notecard drafts.

Mr. Ryan, it occurs to me now, is a keeper.

He was an outsider too: the only time he appears in the video is when he waves to his own reflection.

My mom,
    the correspondent,

Office Depot
Copy paper

CARDINALS   is also keeper.

Mary Karr says of SPEAK, MEMORY,
that for Nabokov, "<u>Nothing</u> in his
existence is banal."

This is true for my mom, who kept meeting agendas
and drafts of her newspaper stories.

It's true for Mr. Ryan, whose video is a reminder
that so much of our time together—of our lives—
happened between games. Moments when
parents and refs shared a patch of shade.

It was true for me and my diaries too.

When I first read them, all I could
see was faulty teenage logic and
unhealthy patterns.

But now I can see that
I was writing toward
a future.
"To remember,"
like Joan Didion,
"what it was to be me."

I even occasionally
addressed my future
self.

I proclaimed I didn't
want kids, but
I addressed
them too.

Although I was often confused and misguided,
I seemed to understand—even then—that
if I just kept WRITING, I'd figure it out.

And now, what if I could
address that old self?

If I could read her
teenage goalkeeper palms?

What would I
tell her?

I would say:
Look at these
HANDS, girl.

They will
save goals,

they will raise
your daughter,

they will
write
your stories.

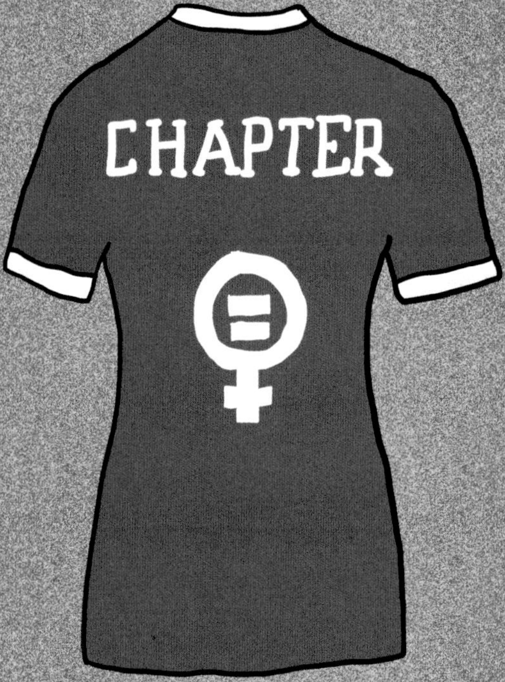
CHAPTER

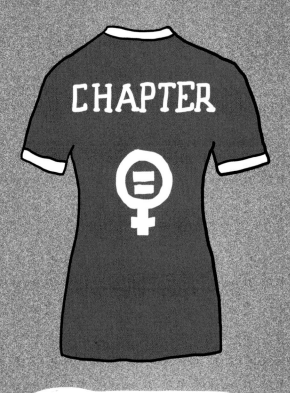

The Revolution

At the end of Lady Florence Dixie's book, as a "stranger in a balloon" flies over 1999 London, he sees "two gleaming gilded statues."

Which gets me thinking of 2 statues unveiled in 2019.

The statue of Brandi Chastain at the Rose Bowl, commemorating the 20th anniversary of her 1999 World Cup goal.

And the statue of
LILY PARR at the
National Football
Museum in Manchester,
honoring the 100th
anniversary of her
joining the
Dick, Kerr Ladies.

We are honoring women
with statues, but, more
than a century later,
have we fulfilled
Lady Dixie's vision
for a feminist REVOLUTION?

Let's take a ride in an
air balloon.

Some things look very good!

The Black Women's Player Collective Is Here to Usher In the Next Generation of Superstar Athletes

Team USA Women Soar at Olympics

Megan Rapinoe among group of "trailblazing" women replacing Victoria's Secret angels

U.S. Women's Soccer Equal Pay Settlement: A Historic Step in a Long Fight for Pay Equity

Canadian Soccer Player Quinn Becomes The First Out Trans And Nonbinary Gold Medalist

Under Miss America 2.0, A Biochemist Takes The Crown

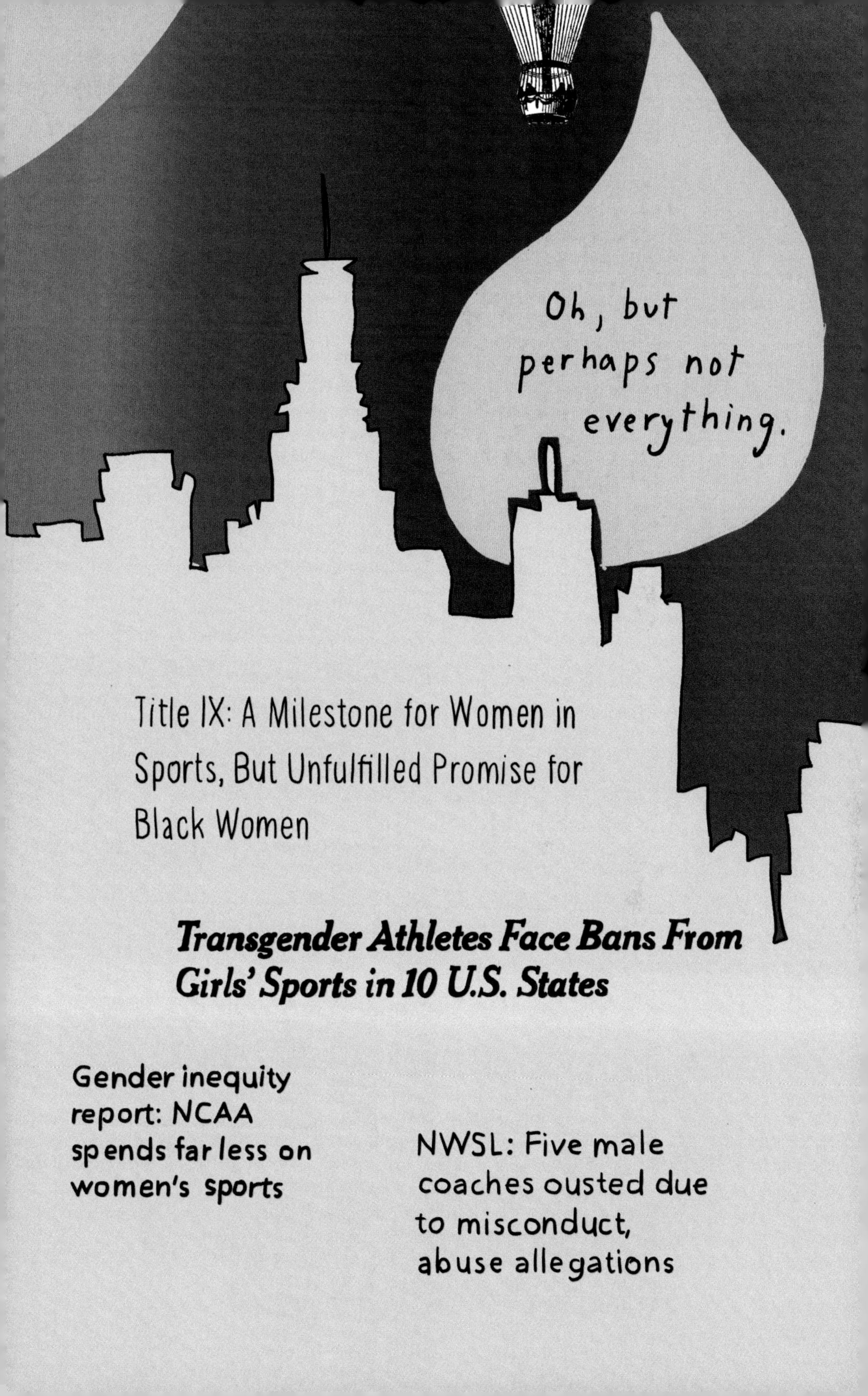
Oh, but perhaps not everything.
Title IX: A Milestone for Women in Sports, But Unfulfilled Promise for Black Women
Transgender Athletes Face Bans From Girls' Sports in 10 U.S. States
Gender inequity report: NCAA spends far less on women's sports
NWSL: Five male coaches ousted due to misconduct, abuse allegations

But women have always responded to injustice by coming together to fight.

We are always
strongest

when we join
together,

support one
another
intersectionally,

= EQUAL PAY

when men
join in →

and when we share our stories.

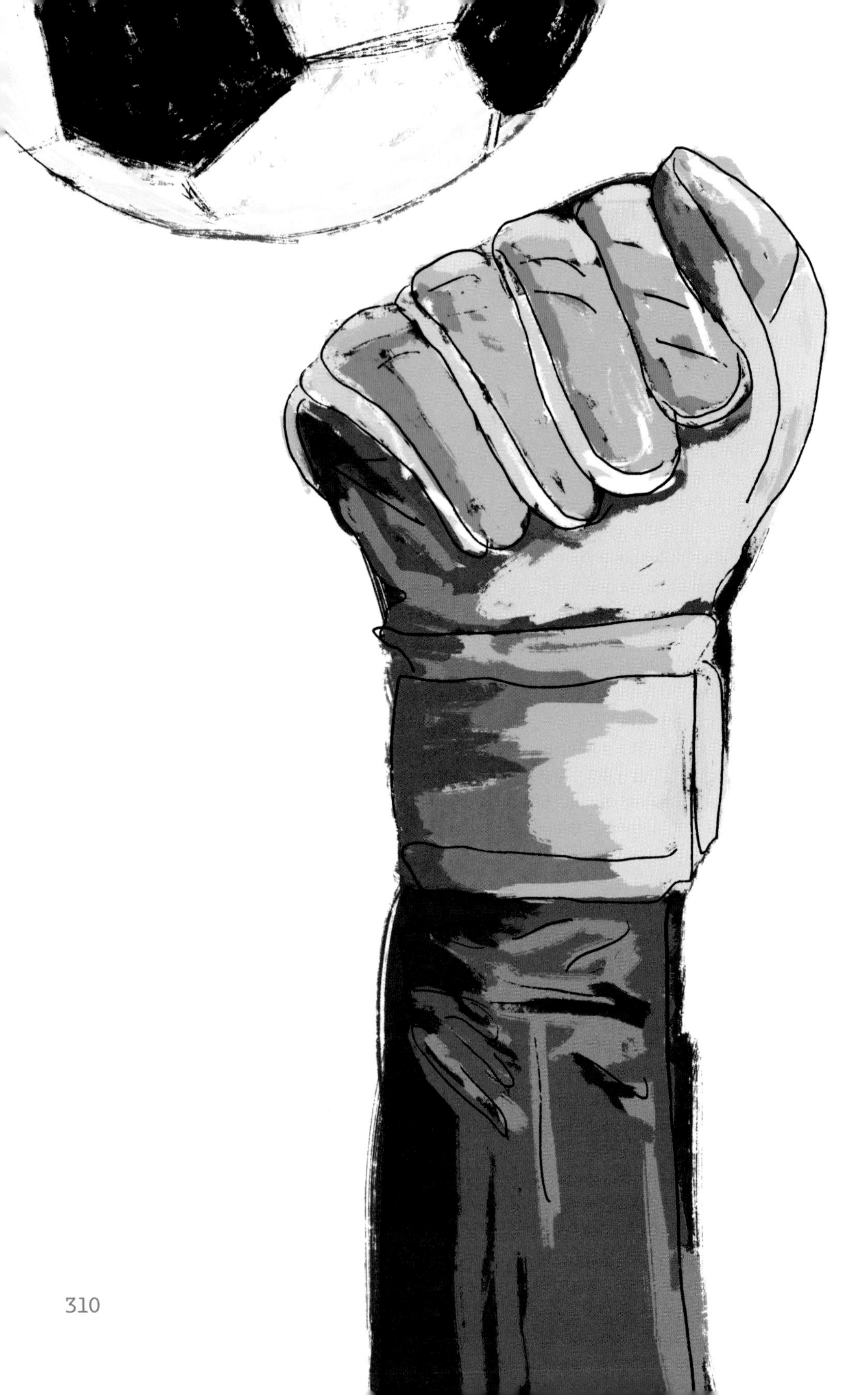

Here's a final story.

For a moment I think
I've time-traveled.

I'd recognize those uniforms
anywhere. Red and white.
Sashes like Miss America.

Excuse me, your team is the Cardinals, right? From Cincinnati?

I played for them too, back in the early days.

Hey, Britt! C'mere. This lady says she was a Cardinal — when did you say?

Oh, a loooong time ago.

We traveled all over together and always came home with a trophy.

I'm babbling.

Seeing her in that familiar uniform has stirred my emotions.

But Britt is looking longingly at her teammates.

Okay, well, good luck!

But, Britt, before you go?

When I was about your age, I wrote something in my diary. It's embarrassing, but it relates to you.

I wrote that I cried because I realized that one day there would be a 1998 Cardinals team and no one would remember "the best ever— '71 Cardinals,"

I cried 3 x's today:
① It started with soccer— Cardinals & how someday it'll be the '98 Cards & no one will remember the best ever— '71 Cardinals

And here you are,
and I was right.

But I'm not crying about it.
Because I think of it differently now,

I've realized that,
whether you were
born in 1998
or 2008 or
2028,

I see you
as my
TEAMMATE.

And aren't we,
Britt?

Even in different uniforms—

across different decades—

aren't we

ALL...

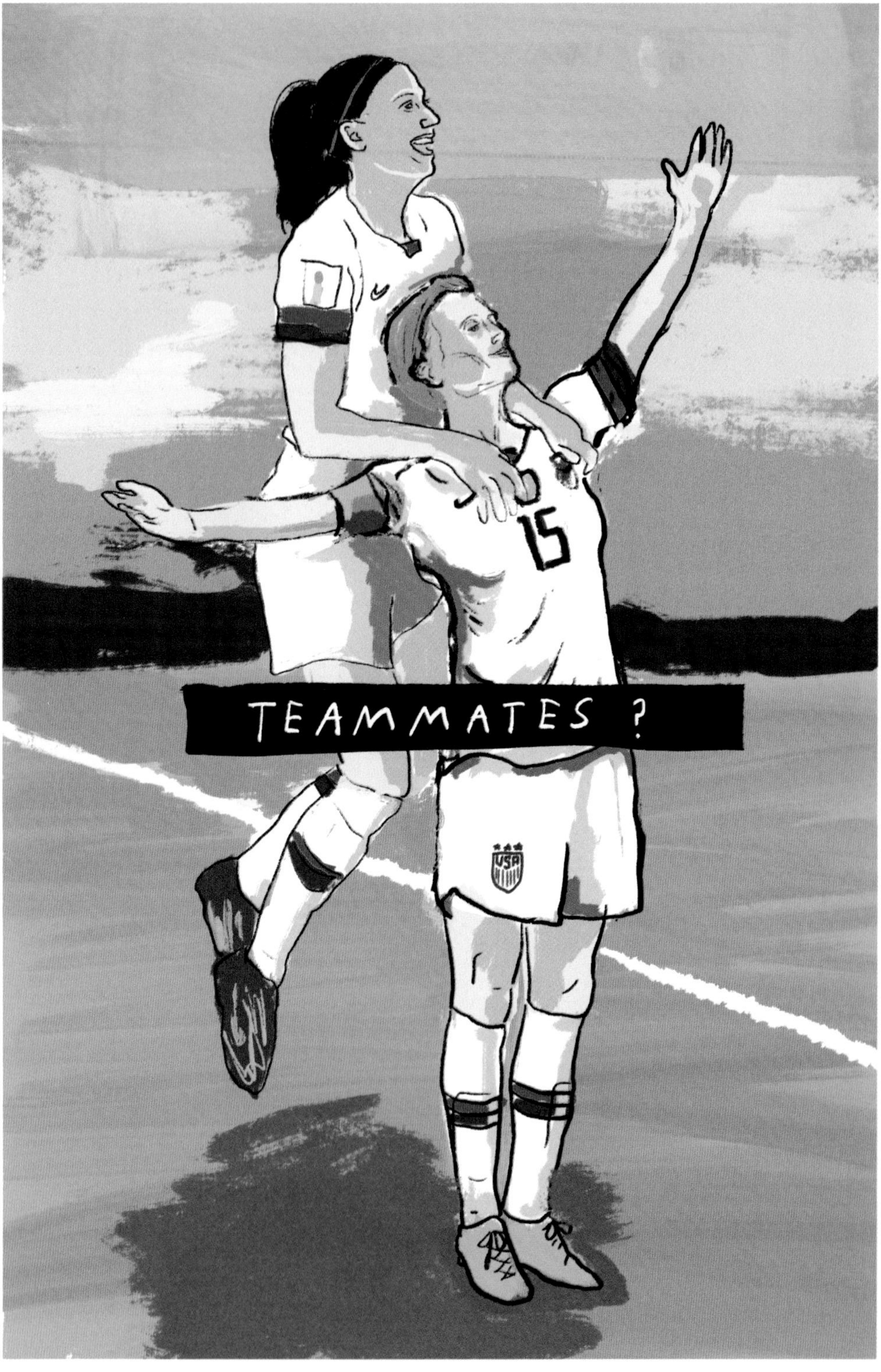
TEAMMATES ?

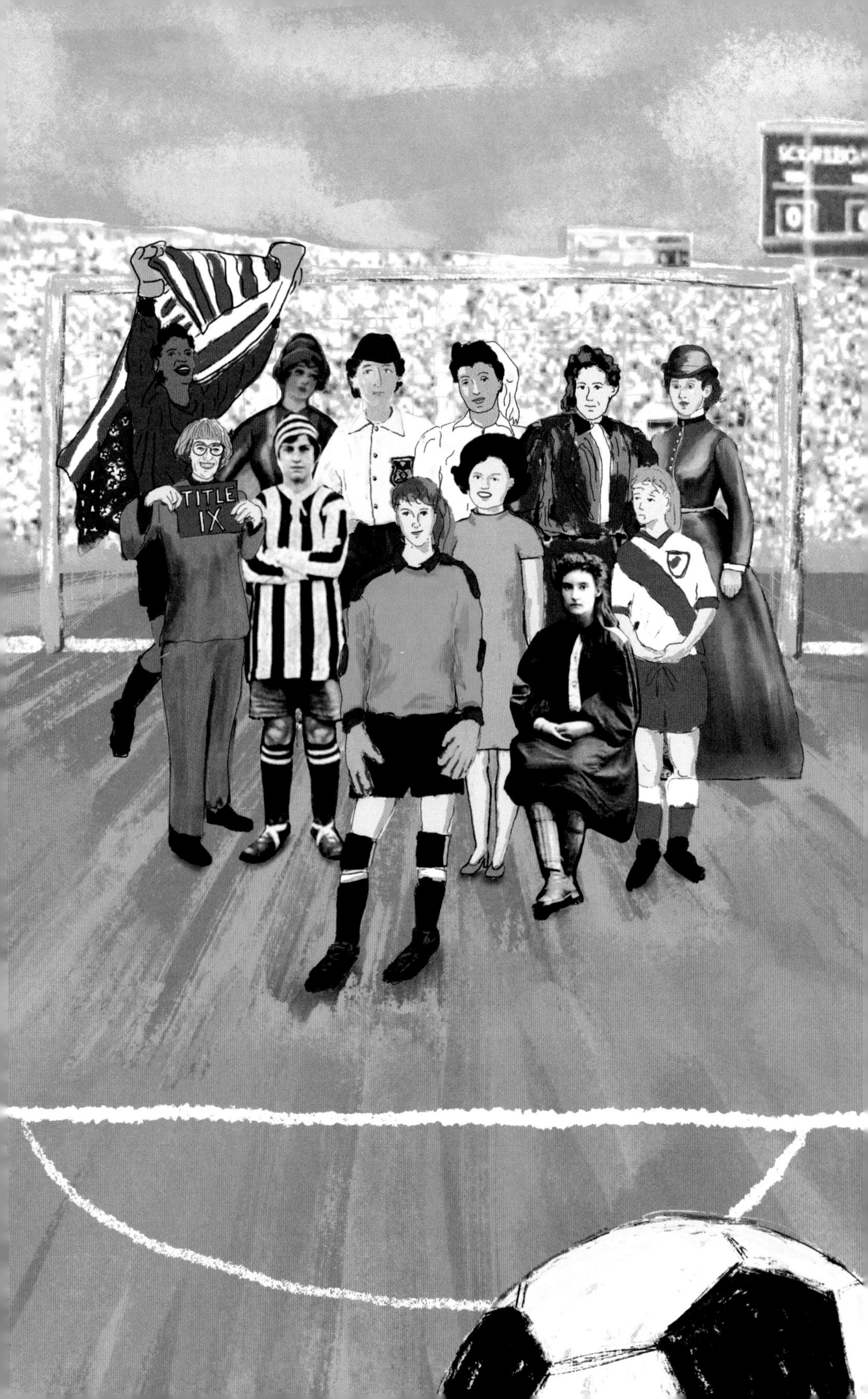
TITLE
IX

About The Author

Kelcey Ervick was born on a snowy April 10, 1971, in Ithaca, New York. She attended Cornell University with her father until the age of two months, at which time she moved to New Jersey until 1977. She then moved to Connecticut and later to Cincinnati where she began her soccer career.

Photo:
Myriam
Nicodemus

Kelcey Ervick is the author of two books about fascinating but not well known women—THE BITTER LIFE OF BOŽENA NĚMCOVÁ and LILIANE'S BALCONY—and the story collection FOR SALE BY OWNER. Her comics have appeared in THE RUMPUS and THE BELIEVER, and she is co-editor with Tom Hart of THE FIELD GUIDE TO GRAPHIC LITERATURE. She lives on the banks of the St. Joseph River and is a professor of English at Indiana University South Bend. Honestly, everything else is in the book.

SOURCES

I consulted and quoted from many sources to tell the stories in this book. Here are some of the main works. For a more extensive list, please visit my website: kelceyervick.com

SPEAK, MEMORY   Vladimir Nabokov

THE NATIONAL TEAM   Caitlin Murray

"Title IX: How We Got It and What a Difference It Made" Bernice Sandler

IN A LEAGUE OF THEIR OWN!   Gail J. Newsham

SOCCERWOMEN   Gemma Clarke

A GAME FOR ROUGH GIRLS   Jean Williams

FROM FOOTBALL TO SOCCER   Brian D. Bunk

SOCCER IN SUN AND SHADOW   Eduardo Galeano
Mark Fried, Trans.

THE GIRLS OF SUMMER   Jere Longman

THE OUTSIDER: A HISTORY OF THE GOALKEEPER Jonathan Wilson

SOLO: A MEMOIR OF HOPE   Hope Solo

ONE LIFE   Megan Rapinoe

GLORIANA; OR, THE REVOLUTION OF 1900. Lady Florence Dixie

A ROOM OF ONE'S OWN   Virginia Woolf

SPECIAL THANKS:
To Steve Bolton and the LIZZY ASHCROFT COLLECTION for Dick, Kerr Ladies images and stories.
And to Dave Ross for the Cardinals video.

ACKNOWLEDGMENTS

Thank you to my agent, Susan Canavan, for believing in this book and in me, and for finding a perfect match in my editor, Lucia Watson, who guided me and championed the manuscript through every stage. I'm so grateful to the entire team at Avery Books: Megan Newman, Suzy Swartz, Lindsay Gordon, Farin Schlussel, Anne Kosmoski, Nellys Liang, Jess Morphew, Rachel Dugan, Sara Johnson, Abby Stubenhofer, and especially Lorie Pagnozzi for the patient art direction.

Thanks to Molly McCaffrey, Sarah Domet, and Jake Mattox, trusted friends and readers, whose insights and intelligence made this a better book. And to the friends who have been a part of the journey: Julie Hernandez, Kristin Czarnecki, Dionne Irving, Aaron Bremyer, David Bell, Tom Hart, and Kelly Schwenkmeyer.

Thanks to my beloved family for their love, laughter, and support: My mom, Janice Bobrovcan; my dad and stepmom, Gary and Pat Ervick; my sister, Darcy Ervick; my brother Dane Ervick and his wife, Melissa, and their boys Xander, Lachlann, and Callum; my brother Travis Ervick and his partner, Hannah Meyer; and in memory of my brother Christian Ervick, whom we all miss so much. Thanks to the Mattox family for welcoming me in and cheering me on.

In a category of her own, thanks to my amazing daughter, Monte Parker, a spirited child who is now a spirited adult.

And to Jake Mattox for your mind, heart, words, and music. And for loving me in a way I didn't know was possible.

A final note of thanks to my 1971 Cardinals teammates and to our parents for all the things we never thanked them for. Thanks to my Xavier teammates, and to my many coaches. Thanks to Sandy Ross. Thanks to "Jen."

Thanks to all the women across generations who have fought for the right to play and for equal pay. Thanks to TITLE IX and those who made it happen. Thanks to the storytellers who preserve women's history.

To the current generation of girl athletes and all those to come: May you build a better future inspired by knowledge of the past.

What's your Title IX story?

Share it at
kelceyervick.com

KEEP IN TOUCH:
@kelcey.parker.ervick
@KelceyErvick